Astrology in the Renaissance

Astrology in the Renaissance

The Zodiac of Life

Eugenio Garin

Translated by Carolyn Jackson and June Allen
Translation revised in conjunction with the author
by Clare Robertson

Routledge & Kegan Paul
London, Boston, Melbourne and Henley

First published in Italian in 1976
by Editori Laterza, Bari, as
Lo Zodiaco Vita
This translation first published in 1983
by Routledge & Kegan Paul Ltd
39 Store Street, London WC1E 7DD,
9 Park Street, Boston, Mass. 02108, USA,
296 Beaconsfield Parade, Middle Park,
Melbourne, 3206, Australia, and
Broadway House, Newtown Road,
Henley-on-Thames, Oxon RG9 1EN
First published as a paperback in 1984
Set in 10/14 Pilgrim by Inforum Ltd, Portsmouth
and printed in Great Britain by
St Edmundsbury Press, Bury St Edmunds, Suffolk

Library of Congress Cataloguing in Publication Data

Garin, Eugenio, 1909–

Astrology in the Renaissance: the zodiac of life
Translation of: Lo zodiaco della vita.
Includes bibliographical references and index.
1. Astrology—History.   2. Renaissance.
I. Title
BF 1676.G3713   1982   133.5   82-13188

ISBN 0-7100-9259-8
ISBN 0-7100-9484-1 Pbk

Contents

Introduction

Tears are Kronos; birth is Zeus; speech [*logos*] is Hermes;
anger is Ares; the moon is sleep; Aphrodite is desire; and the
sun is laughter, for by him laugh all mortal minds, and the
boundless universe.

(Hermes, *On Destiny* (Stobeus, I, 5, 14; fr. Herm.29),
(tr. W. Scott, *Hermetica*, vol.I, p.533, Oxford, 1924)

In the introduction to the first volume of the invaluable
Catalogus codicum astrologorum Graecorum, written in
1898, Franz Cumont made a series of important observations.
He underlined above all the enormous amount of 'astrological' material lying unexplored in libraries, neglected and
scorned. He pointed out the importance of being wary of the
'pitfalls', especially those of the *clarissima inventa*, when
one wants to understand the process of the human search for
'truth'. Cumont had in mind not only Greek astrological texts
(and those dealing with magic and alchemy): he also clearly
saw the origins of Egyptian, Chaldean and Indian cultures
and the echoes of Arabic medieval tradition, as well as Latin
and Byzantine traditions, in them. He was aware that astrological literature is interwoven with religious and scientific
thought, mythical and rational themes, and that it mirrors
real events and fantastic transfigurations. Some years later,
in 1905, at the Paris conference on 'Eastern religions in

Roman paganism', he expounded on 'the religious nature
of astrology which is always maintained at the expense of
logic', because 'planets and constellations were not only
cosmic forces whose propitious or inauspicious actions
brought weakness or strength according to the cycles of a
path fixed by eternity; they were divinities which could see
and understand, which brought gladness or grief, had a voice
and a sex, were fertile or sterile, gentle or fierce, subservient
or dominating.' The precise classifications and distinctions in
use at that time, between an astrology which was 'religious'
and an astrology which was 'scientific', did not hold up
because people kept finding the echoes of ancient beliefs
within even the most coherent of mathematical treatises. It
was natural that, as fast as the volumes of the *Catalogus*
followed one after another (and with them those of the
alchemical codices), references from one field to another and
from one age to the next increased, and so texts written
recently revealed themselves to be faithful reproductions of
ancient models. Thus, concluded Cumont, it is precisely
because of the complexity of astrological themes, and their
ability to be so eclectic, that one cannot investigate the
origins of beliefs and of sciences without looking in depth at
the work of the astrologers, who often did no more than
project worldly events into the heavens and astral images.

In 1937, almost forty years later (there were by then seven-
teen parts of the *Catalogus*), Cumont published a fascinating
book in Brussels, valuable to historians as well as to 'philosophers' (that is, presuming there are philosophers who read
these books). It is worth recounting the book's history. Wil-
helm Gundel, the famous scholar of the history of astrology,
who in 1936 published *Dekane und Dekansternbilder* in the
Studien of the Warburg Institute, had identified a *Liber
Hermetis Trismegisti* in a Latin manuscript of the Renais-

sance (MS. Harley 3731, dated 1431). This was an astrological compilation translated from the Greek of the Alexandrian period, some parts of which can be traced back to the third century BC. Gundel published the text with a full commentary in Munich in 1936, in the Bavarian Academy of Sciences *Abhandlungen*. No one knew about any other volumes of the work, though the fact that it had a wide circulation in the Middle Ages is proved by the fact that there remains a version of an important chapter written in Picard dialect. This was to be found in a Parisian volume originally written for Marie of Luxembourg (who died in 1324). Gundel's analysis showed the importance of the *Liber Hermetis* for the reconstruction of ancient astrology, from the doctrine of the thirty-six divine decans, which divide the 360 degrees of the sphere, to the numbering of the seventy-two fixed stars which seemed to be connected with Hipparchus's catalogue. But the work carried out by Cumont is perhaps even more relevant, and certainly more interesting. It was based on lengthy research (from Boll to Kroll) into Latin and Greek astrological texts, from Vettius Valens to Firmicus Maternus. Cumont was convinced that at the end of antiquity, 'as the critical faculty grew weak, the content of such ancient books was faithfully reproduced and was venerated as the apocalypse of a divine wisdom' – 'divina secreta . . . quae in libris mysticis insunt' ('divine secrets which are contained in mystical books'). In this way Cumont reconstructed through the *Liber Hermetis* and the documents linked to it an eloquent picture of the social and moral conditions of Hellenistic Egypt. As the astrologer had projected human events into the heavens in order to identify their underlying rhythms and hidden patterns on a 'divine' plane, so the historian brings them back to earth from heaven and restores their original dimensions of dates, references and events. Demons and gods, stars and celestial images are re-

placed with the king and the court, condottieri and function-
aries, artisans and traders, learned men and priests. This is a
complete and accurate picture, even down to the problems of
public security, to the threat of brigands in the countryside
and all other aspects of daily life. Indeed, one asked the
astrologer for predictions about the outcome of journeys,
about the possibilities of recovering stolen goods, catching
scoundrels or handling courtesans. On this subject Cumont
also commented that 'Doctors of the sidereal sciences, and
even the austere Ptolemy, dedicate entire pages to listing all
the aberrations of a morbid eroticism with the calm shame-
lessness of casuists'. Astrologers seek the causes and explanations for men's peculiarities in the stars, as they would for
curious phenomena in nature, and so they are written down
in their treatises. 'Incontinentes enim in vitiis fiunt propter
Venerum . . .' ('For they become incontinent in their vices
because of Venus . . .') – says the *Liber Hermetis* – 'quae
virorum et mulierum omnimodi perficit coitus, matri-
monia et conventiones . . . facit fornicatores et fornicatrices
turpia facientes' ('who brings about all kinds of unions of
men and women, marriages and contracts . . . she makes
fornicators and whores who do shameful deeds'). One can
read a whole chapter of Egyptian life in the stella-images, as
Cumont did, and while this documents the unity of a conception of the world based on a precise correspondence between heaven and earth, between macrocosm and microcosm, it also demonstrates, besides, its ambiguous nature, the
need for an exhaustive study of astrology in order to have an
adequate knowledge of the past: of all the epochs in which it
flourished, or was prevalent, or was discussed and entered
into crisis.[1]

Ancient astrology was the converging point for various
themes and could be looked at under many contrasting

aspects (one need only think of the difference between genethlialogy and 'cathartic' astrology, or between the theory of a determinism starting at birth, or conception, and hypotheses about the possibility of choice at certain times based on a knowledge of the horoscope). Undoubtedly it showed itself to be linked originally to a geocentric vision of a finite universe where the celestial spheres, through their perfection, are superior to the sublunar world which is causally subordinated to them: where a 'divine' heaven is the source of movement and light, of heat and life. But if this was in fact the core of Hellenistic astrology, which fully re-emerged in the Renaissance period, one cannot state absolutely (as has been done again recently by David Pingree in the article on 'Astrology' in the *Dictionary of the History of Ideas*) that as 'astrology is the study of the impact of the celestial bodies . . . upon the sublunar world' it 'presupposes a geocentric and finite universe'. George Sarton, who also called for the intervention of the secular arm against the astrologers of today, in one of the Montgomery lectures given in 1954 at the University of Nebraska,[2] emphasised that: 1 the claims of astrology are independent of whether the earth or the sun is placed at the centre of the planetary system; 2 astrology did not disappear after the acceptance of the Copernican system but continued to grow abundantly; 3 Kepler himself not only compiled horoscopes, but countered the critics of Pico with: 'constantissima (quantum in naturalibus sperari potest) experientia de commotione sublunarium naturarum sub conjunctiones et aspectus Erronum', that 'edocuit et reluctantem vicit'. ('Most constant (in so far as can be hoped for in natural things) experience of the disturbance of sublunary natures under the conjunctions and aspects of the Planets', that 'taught and overcame him despite his reluctance.') And besides, he asked himself, why deny that the stars and the heavens have different influences through their radiations, 'ut objecta movent sensus, lux oculus, sonus auditum, calor tactum' ('as objects move the senses, as light the eyes, sound the hearing, warmth the sense of touch')?[3] The important thing is that the *constantissima experientia* proves that there are basic and 'true' laws and structures, substituting them for the illusions of capricious and *ad hoc* powers. Cassirer recalls the debate between Kepler and Patrizi in *The Philosophy of Symbolic Forms*. Patrizi held that the efforts of mathematical astronomy to determine the course of planets through the various inter-linking orbits (cycles and epicycles) were in vain as the planets were nothing more than demonic beings which pass through the ether at changing speeds and with different and strangely tortuous paths. For Kepler mathematical astrology ought to discover the true causes of the perceptible illusion by distinguishing their actual movements and by defining 'the simplicity and the ordered regularity of their orbit'. There is nothing to stop one thinking that behind the mythical and religious fantasies of the 'influences' and 'images' lies a rational plan, which can be strictly calculated and defined according to the principles of scientific knowledge – as in fact Ptolemy had wanted to do in the *Tetrabiblos*. This is an age-long debate which Aby Warburg summed up very well: astrology is the meeting and confrontation point between the demands of a rational order, as in Greek science, and the myths and superstitions inherited from the East: between logic and magic, between mathematics and mythology, between Athens and Alexandria. Goethe was right when he said that the 'majority of that which is called superstition is born from a mistaken application of mathematics', and Aby Warburg added that 'the modern scientist always wavers between magical practice and cosmological mathematics.'[4]

But it is not an easy task to save Athens from Alexandria because it is difficult to see where Athens finishes and Alexandria begins. It is not easy to trace the boundaries between the rationality of a law of nature and the 'irrational' yet effective and real force of a prayer or exorcism. Ptolemy and Copernicus, Aristarchus and Galileo, seemed unable to exorcise the sad influence of Saturn, and the ambiguous shadow of Pythagoras seems to linger over all physico-mathematical knowledge. The truth is that the conception of human science is never perfect, and pure reason shows itself in turn to be a pure myth, or an ideology: or at best a regulative idea, in the Kantian sense.

So, the debate on astrology at the beginning of the modern age, when science was beginning to define its methods in the crisis of the ancient conceptions of the world, which were either waning or coming to life again, is an exemplary document of this impossible problem of theory and practice, of concepts and sentiments, of myths and reasoning. It is indeed because astrology was an all-encompassing, global concept, due to the multiplicity of its aspects, that the debate about its themes came to touch every human activity. On the other hand, in the comparison of the various positions with each other, their limits and contradictions were also revealed. If the struggle against a fate determined by the stars seems a valid vindication of man's free action, it is also true that the defenders of the most rigorous determinism show a keen sense of the rationality of natural laws and of the unity of nature. 'The fates rule the world, everything stands fixed by law.' ('Fata regunt orbem, certa stant omnia lege.') So, if the fight against superstition and magic rituals seems to reveal an enlightened rationalism, the appeal to the senses and passions (and to all the deep physical forces which are denied to the conscious mind, dreams and abnormal states) not only emphasises the existence of real forces and unexplored realms of experience, but also foreshadows some of the more fruitful undertakings of modern research.

Bringing into focus the discussions of the 'conjunctionists', the supporters of the 'great cycles', the alternations between religions and civilisations, helps, therefore, an understanding of the roots of the new philosophies of history, and puts in perspective, beside Vico's cycles and recycles, the themes and problems of more recent thought. At the same time one sees the great problems of human thought appearing again in new forms: nature and its laws, the meaning and the place of man in the cosmos, the value and the use of mathematical tools, the rhythms and contradictions of experience. At the same time one can identify the connection between scientific research, political and religious life and artistic production. The 'living' statues of great art and the development of the theory of 'imitation' transpose 'magical' languages onto another plane. And it illustrates the tortuousness of the path of 'science' and its struggle to become established amid continual illusions and inappropriate expansions. In a well-known passage Mach once wrote:

> The French encyclopaedists of the eighteenth century imagined they were not far from a final explanation of the world by physical and mechanical principles . . . and we can deeply sympathize with this expression of intellectual joy, so unique in history. But now, after a century has elapsed, after our judgement has grown more sober, the world-conception of the encyclopaedists appears to us as a *mechanical mythology* in contrast to the *animistic* of the old religions. Both views contain undue and fantastical exaggerations of an incomplete perception.

Unfortunately, without these arbitrary conclusions, without these fanciful visions of a 'whole', human research cannot proceed. Even Mach, in this context, expounded his own theory, which had no sounder foundation than the others, be they astrological, animistic or hermetic. He believed that following 'the economy of a sound mind', humanity should be able to 'approach, slowly, gradually, but surely to . . . a unified view of the world'. But, he honestly confessed that: 'The highest philosophy of the scientific investigator is . . . this toleration of an incomplete conception of the world and the preference for it rather than an apparently perfect, but inadequate, conception.'[5] The discussion about astrology, which raged with such bitterness at the dawn of modern science, helps to put in focus the reciprocal relationship between visions of the world and researches which are specific and concrete, and, at the same time, the complex and ambiguous nature of the very same astrological positions.

The following pages faithfully reproduce four lectures given at the Collège de France in April and May 1975. Only some bibliographical notes have been added; the text is unchanged from what was said and expressly preserves the modest tone of the lectures. Detailed examples and documented discussions have been omitted from this text as the author has dealt with them in other works. These notes are simply the conclusions of that previous research.

Special thanks are due to André Chastel who promoted these lectures and to whom the author feels bound by a long friendship and the closeness of their work. Sincere thanks to Marcel Bataillon and Marie-Thérèse d'Alverny for their kind attention and valuable suggestions.

Florence, April 1975 – January 1976   E.G.

Chapter 1

Astrology and history: Albumasar and the 'Great Conjunctions'

It is almost a commonplace of recent historiography that one could, in the Renaissance, make a precise distinction in astrology between two aspects which had previously, in antiquity and the Middle Ages, been inextricably linked and were indeed frequently confused under the one category 'astrology': the first being the religious and superstitious aspect, the second analytical and scientific. So, prophetic astrology, or, as the Arabs called it, the 'science, or art, of the laws of the stars', or the 'science of the laws' (in Latin the *scientia iudiciorum stellarum*, the science of the judgments of the stars; hence *astrologia iudiciaria*, judiciary astrology, or *astronomia iudiciorum*, astronomy of the judgments, was finally to be isolated and definitively superseded by mathematical astrology, in other words astronomy (*astrologia quadrivialis* or *doctrinalis*).[1]

In fact, Ptolemy, in the introduction to the *Tetrabiblos*, or *Quadripartitum*, had already perceptively observed that the science of the stars consists of two parts. The first, both in order and importance, studies the shape and appearance of the Sun and Moon's movements (*schematismus ton chineseon*), as well as the celestial bodies in general, in terms of their reciprocal relationship with the earth. The second is based on the physical qualities of these forms and tries to predict the events of the world in which we live. Only the first, with its demonstrative method, is really an autonomous science and desirable in itself beyond any practical results. On this subject Ptolemy refers us to the *Almagest* in which he had systematically set out mathematical astrology. The second, dependent on the first, though less rigorous in its methods, is concerned instead with events in the sublunar world which it tries to forecast with maximum probability from the celestial configurations.[2] Ibn Khaldun commented with great clarity: '[Astrology] . . . is all guesswork and conjectures based upon the [assumed existence of] astral influence, and a resulting conditioning of the air.' But Ibn Khaldun also distinguishes between the true and proper thesis of Ptolemy on the physical effects of the positions and radiations of the stars and the astrologers' hypothesis of supernatural influences and perceptions. As he refuted, with a vigorous rationalism, the inclusion of the supernatural, whether in the form of planetary influence or in the form of a gift of divination, he reduced the work of astrologers to the level of pure conjecture and guesswork: 'If it [astrology] were established [as a fact], it would, at best, be guessing and conjecturing. It has nothing whatever to do with [super-natural perception] . . .'[3]

Ibn Khaldun's *Prolegomena* take us to the end of the four-teenth century and the work seems to parallel the process of the scientific rationalisation of astronomy, of which we spoke with reference to Western culture. Going back to the research of Aby Warburg, Ernst Cassirer wrote in 1927 in his famous book, *The Individual and the Cosmos in Renaissance Philosophy*:

Astrology, from its very inception, presents a double intellectual front. As a theory, it seeks to place before us

the eternal laws of the universe in clear outline; whereas
its practice stands under the sign of the fear of demons, the
'most primitive form of religious causation'. (tr. M. Don-
andi, New York, 1963, p.105)

So according to Cassirer, the value of some of the great
critical and polemical works written during the fifteenth and
sixteenth centuries was that they distinguished these separate aspects. By looking at the heavens and the stars and their
motions and radiations, these works eradicated all trace of
astral cults, and so established the basis of a rational and
scientific vision, purely physico-mathematical: modern astronomy. Cassirer even says of the *De naturalium effectuum
causis sive incantationibus* by Pietro Pomponazzi completed in 1520:

> Although [it] . . . is still within the ambit of the astrolog-
> ical view, it nevertheless executes a sharp and conscious
> *separation* between these two basic moments of theory and
> practice, which hitherto had been inextricably inter-
> twined. Therein lies the intellectual and historical signi-
> ficance of the work . . . The purely 'primitive', the demonic
> element in astrology is removed, and in its place remains
> only the thought of the one, inviolable regularity of occur-
> rences, recognizing no exceptions and no accidents: the
> demonic causality of faith gives way to the causality of
> science . . . the astrological concept of causality is replaced
> by that of mathematics and physics. (Ibid., pp. 105f)

Cassirer subsequently wrote, though in reference to another
work – the famous *Disputationes adversus astrologiam
divinatricem* by Giovanni Pico della Mirandola, written
almost a century before and which perhaps constitutes the
climax of the polemic on astrology:[4]

> Pico goes beyond a mere criticism of astrology; he draws a
> sharp line separating the magical signs of astrology from

3

the intellectual signs of mathematics and mathematical physics. Now the way is clear for an interpretation of the 'cipher writing' of nature through mathematical physical symbols which are at the same time conceived as symbols. They no longer confront the mind as strange powers but as its own creations.

Is Cassirer stating what was really the case, or were the polemics surrounding astrology much more complicated and divided? Was modern physico-mathematical science really born through this rigorous process of pure rationalisation and an outright refutation of magical and demonical elements, of occult forces and mysterious powers, of hidden links and enigmatic attractions? Aby Warburg recalled the arguments of Luther who bluntly declared to the humanist Philip Melanchthon, the 'Dominus Doctor', in August 1540: 'No one will persuade me, neither Paul nor an Angel from Heaven, nor yet Philip, to believe in the divinations of astrology which are wrong so often that there can be nothing less trustworthy.'[5] Luther, like Savonarola and his disciple Pico, was primarily inspired by a religious and moral passion rather than by scientific demands. He fought the notion of a fate determined by the stars, in the name of man's free will, which is subject not to nature but to God. But, in their battle, they did not align themselves with the 'new men', the humanists. On the contrary, it was the humanists who were above all their adversaries, be they poets like Pontano, or thinkers like Melanchthon. It is certainly no coincidence that the impressionable Ficino, though a 'pious philosopher', was susceptible to all the temptations of astrology, and at the same time stellar symbols and divinities were featuring more and more frequently in the poetry, frescoes, customs and the political writings of the Renaissance. These were certainly different to those of the Middle Ages, and they reflected the

harmonious forms of their most ancient sources – Oriental,
Greek and Egyptian, but they were certainly no less deceptive: they were merely gods of the heavens and not frightening
demons. In other words the battle surrounding astrology
touched on every aspect of culture. The dispute was lengthy
and was fought along unclear and imprecise lines, clouded by
all sorts of ambiguity. Nor can one be sure if the two works
cited above, which Cassirer analyses as exemplary, Pico's
Disputationes and Pomponazzi's *De incantationibus*, which
are presented as if they belonged to the same school and were
fighting on the same side – scientific reason against superstition – were not in fact in conflict with each other. Pomponazzi in the *De incantationibus* violently attacks and
indeed scornfully rejects Pico, and bitterly defends astrology
in the name of science, accusing Pico of a complete lack of
any form of scientific rigour.[6] Without a doubt, the words
of Pomponazzi are not to be taken literally, and there are
certainly many deep similarities between the two works,
both of which were influential in Europe until the end of the
seventeenth century. But certainly things are less simple
than Cassirer, and others with him, state. The processes
through which modern science came to be established are
certainly less clear-cut and much more protracted, especially
when one tries to define its method and to identify the notion
of physical causality. The stages of so-called 'scientific progress' are anything but straightforward and unambiguous,
and for a long time they have in fact been mixed up with all
kinds of magical, hermetic and mystical themes. Even in the
middle of the eighteenth century, G.M. Bose, Professor of
Philosophy and Dean of the University of Wittenburg, wrote,
with regard to Newton and the Theory of Universal Attraction: 'Actio per distans dabitur? Tunc impediesne/ Quo
minus in distans stella Talisman agat?/ Gaude Melanchton,

redeunt horoscopus, Haly,/ Almutec, Athacir, Alcecadenor, Hylec./ Actio per distans dabitur? Mox thessala rugis/ horrida setosis, quam furibunda! redit.' ('Shall action at a distance be granted? Will you then prevent a star from acting as a Talisman at a distance? Rejoice Melanchthon, the horoscope returns, Haly, Almutec, Athacir, Alcecadenor, Hylec. Shall action at a distance be granted? Soon the Thessalian witch, horrid with wrinkles and bristles, raging, shall return.')[7] With Newton and 'action at a distance', it seemed to Professor Bose that ultimately, at the height of the eighteenth century, Melanchthon and the astrological tradition, together with talismanic magic and the theory of *sympathia rerum* (the sympathy of matter) had finally triumphed over Pico and Galileo.

However, that is not to say that one wishes to agree with Professor Bose's less than elegant distichs; one wants to underline not only the complexity of the problem but also the difficulties involved in outlining the debates surrounding astrology during the Renaissance, in which art and science, religion and philosophy began, not by chance, to converge or to conflict. This lasted for almost three centuries until the triumph of the so-called 'scientific revolution' which definitively closed the debate. In other words, while it is necessary to eliminate the idea that a complete rupture took place between modern astronomy and medieval astrology during the Renaissance, it is most important to be aware of the wide dissemination of astrological, magical and hermetic themes at the beginning of modern culture and their persistence everywhere in the most varied forms, not only in the images of art but also in the new science itself. It is worth quoting, as a prelude to the attempt to carry out a more adequate historical investigation, a unique document, taken from the writings of Galileo's followers.[8]

6

On 14 July 1642, Bonaventura Cavalieri wrote a very melancholic and significant letter from Bologna to Evangelista Torricelli. He spoke of the lack of public interest in physico-mathematical sciences and of their lack of success in the practical field. While rigorous research, and in particular mathematics, was not exciting any interest, judicial astrology was widely popular. A new Archimedes could be born – lamented Cavalieri – and no one would take any notice of him, while the most charlatan of astrologers could find honours, money and power everywhere. Cavalieri says that: 'Poor mathematicians, and above all geometers, after endless effort' cannot even dream about 'the glorious fame' achieved by the interpreters of the stars. In short, as mathematical science is useless in its practical application to everyday life, it holds no interest. It is advisable, therefore, at least for the 'extrinsic end' as Cavalieri called it, to adapt oneself to the opinions and demands of the majority, and to make horoscopes and prophecies, while keeping rigorous science for oneself, 'for one's own end', and for those 'who prefer knowledge to semblance'.

There is no need to distinguish between these two people who were among the most celebrated of Galileo's followers. The one an illustrious mathematician, the other a great physicist, both took part in a European debate which had as its protagonists Galileo and Kepler, Mersenne and Gassendi, Pascal and Descartes, and later, on the very subject of Cavalieri's 'indivisibles', Leibniz and Newton. Nevertheless, faced with the survival of divinatory astrology, and all that it imported from hermeticism and magic, and from general beliefs and conceptions, they seemed to submit, these pupils of the same Galileo who, though he did not open the way to 'action at a distance' and to lunar influences, had not hesitated to elaborate a theory of the tides which was absolutely untenable. In fact, reading this resigned and disheartened capitulation by scientists of such prominence in the middle of the seventeenth century, one has the impression that, at least on the level of public opinion and habits, and perhaps also on that of practical application, of beliefs and of moral life, the anti-astrological debate finished in defeat. This was the very same debate which, about three centuries before, the newly-born humanism had opened when, in the words of Petrarch, man's freedom and dignity had been re-established against a fate determined by the stars, and rationality had replaced superstition and magical beliefs. Petrarch had written with a simple classical elegance:[9]

> Leave free the paths of truth and of life . . . These globes of fire cannot be guides for us . . . The virtuous souls, stretching forward to their sublime destiny, shine with a more beautiful inner light. Illuminated by these rays, we have no need of these swindling astrologers and lying prophets who empty the coffers of their credulous followers of gold, who deafen their ears with nonsense, corrupt judgment with their errors, and disturb our present life and make people sad with false fears of the future.

Petrarch was writing in about 1362 while the plague was raging in Padua and obscure omens were accompanying a great disaster. As always the astrologers were reducing the catastrophic earthly events to unusual influences of the stars; only the heavens from which comes the light and warmth of the Sun, giving life to all, could be the source of general death. Petrarch, who saw all the dangers of stellar determinism and feared the destruction of the freedom of human initiative through an indiscriminate natural necessity, started something which was to become on the one hand a radical criticism of heavenly causality and on the other an analysis of superstitious beliefs of ancient origin.

On the other hand, the melancholy conclusions of Bonaventura Cavalieri do not imply the futility of almost three
centuries of 'humanistic' debate. If, after Copernicus had
completely revolutionised the structure of the cosmos, Kepler
and Graz had still to adapt themselves once again to casting
horoscopes, this only means that the origins of modern
science did not come either from a radical break or from an
instantaneous enlightenment. In order to define the progress
of astronomy and the crisis of astrology one must bring into
focus the whole complexity of themes which characterise the
investigations of the humanistic origins of the Renaissance
and the great scientific epoch of the late seventeenth century. Besides, Kepler himself, who certainly did not believe in
the validity of 'predictions', believed openly in the existence
of the soul of the Sun ('animam quoque . . in corpore Solis
inesse necesse est' ('it is necessary that there should be a soul
too . . . in the body of the Sun)) and the inner life of the world
('mundus totus anima plenus' ('the whole world is filled with
life')) not to mention the existence of celestial powers. And if
he appreciated, at least in part, Pico's arguments in the
Disputationes, on which he proposed to comment, he still did
not accept their radicalism, which was not exclusively made
up of scientific reasoning. On the contrary, he accepted some
of the themes central to astrology, such as the theory of
'aspects' ('cognatio aspectibus cum consonantiis musicis'
('the affinity of the aspects with musical harmonies')) and
for this reason he considered the arguments of Pico to be
insufficient: ('denique fecit liber refutando nonnulla, ut iis
ego fidem adhiberem, quibus antea, ut fidem derogarem,
astrologi defendendo effecerant. Sic fuit cum Aspectibus'
('finally the book proceeded by refuting some things, so that I
might put faith in those things which the astrologers had
previously defended in order that I might withdraw my faith.

So it was with the Aspects'.))[10] He continued: 'a constant experience – as much as one can hope for in the field of physical phenomena – had convinced [him], despite his reluctance, of the influence of the conjunctions on the sub-lunar world.' Galileo himself, a constant adversary of divinatory astrology, made somewhat strange affirmations about the Sun and light. One seems to hear echoes of solar cults in his words; nor is it rare to come across neoplatonic beliefs and theories, even in his work, which creep in among mathematical proofs. His famous letter to Monsignor Pietro Dini, of 23 March 1615, which made full use of the Psalm *Deus in Sole posuit latibulum suum*, and with extensive reference to pseudo-Dionysian metaphysics of light, demonstrates the difficulty of separating that which is mathematical and physical from that which is metaphysical and mystical within the realm of rigorous Galilean astronomy. And it is Galileo who tells us that, 'before the creation of the Sun, the spirit with its heat and prolific qualities' came to give life to matter ('*foventem aquas*' ('warming the waters')): 'so that we can truthfully assert that this life-giving spirit and this light which spread throughout the world came together and was united and strengthened in the solar body, and being placed in the centre of the universe, was thus made more splendid and vigorous, shining out its light anew.' In other words the Sun, according to Galileo, is the mediator between the primordial light, source of life, and the living universe. The original light, physically contracted in the Sun, explodes from it and spreads to all points of the universe. From this follows the thesis that the 'splendour of the Sun' is 'a meeting point in the centre of the world for the lights of the stars which are spherically placed around it. They emit their rays which meet and intersect in the centre where they grow and increase their light a thousandfold; so that the light thus

strengthened is reflected and spreads itself rather more vigor-
ously, full of virile, so to speak, and lively heat, and so gives
life to all the bodies which orbit its centre; so that it is rather
like the heart of an animal in which there is a continual
regeneration of the vital spirits, which sustain and give life to
all its members . . . just as the Sun, while nourished from
without, sustains the source from which this light and prolific
heat continually emanate, which gives life to all the bodies
which surround it.'[11] The quotation from the famous text of
Galileo could be continued; it would be both instructive and
surprising at the same time. Anyway it demonstrates the
presence of all kinds of echoes in the scientist's work: next
to the metaphysics of neoplatonic origin there is even the
cabbalistic theme of the concentration of light and its explosive radiations. But more interesting is the translation
into astrological language of the 'strengthening' of rays
according to where they meet, and of their intersection,
fragmentation and augmentation operating positively. '*Ut
Gigas, ut fortis*' ('Like a Giant, like a strong man'), the Sun
projects its radiations, 'which work effectively and have the
power to penetrate all other bodies, and which can also move
through immense spaces with the greatest speed, being the
almost instantaneous emanation of light.' The same sun-
heart correlation on which Galileo insisted, and with which
William Harvey opened his *Exercitatio anatomica de motu
cordis* (Anatomical essay on the movement of the heart)
('cor animalium, fundamentum . . . vitae, princeps omnium, microcosmi sol . . .' ('the animal's heart is the basis of
its life, its chief member, the sun of its microcosm . . .'), tr.
K.J. Franklin, Oxford, 1957, p.3), is simply a commonplace
inherited from medieval astrological literature. Pietro
d'Abano in his *Lucidator*, when discussing the celestial
position of the sun, and its place between Mars and Venus,

makes the observation: 'Sol est in celo sicut cor, ut aiunt, in animali. Est enim secundum Platonem celum velut animal quoddam magnum, sed in eo cor secundum medium situatur de partibus tamquam regnans in regno ut undique possit . . . circumspicere.' ('The sun is in the heavens just as the heart, so they say, is in animals. For according to Plato the sky is like some huge animal but its heart is situated in the middle of its parts, like a ruler in his kingdom, so that he can . . . look in all directions.')[12] It is almost superfluous to emphasise here the other recurrent link between *Sol-Rex* ('Sun' and 'King'), or *princeps: Sol-Rex (princeps) cor* ('Ruler: Sun-King (Ruler) heart'). On the other hand, Pietro Pomponazzi, in his commentary to the *Meteore* written in 1522, preserved in his fuller *reportatio* (account) in the Latin manuscript 6535 of the Bibliothèque Nationale in Paris, declares himself to be incompetent in astrology ('ego non intelligo astrologiam' ('I do not understand astrology')) and he exclaimed at a certain point in his lectures *de generatione et corruptione* (1519): 'Homo est microcosmus, idest parvus mundus, unde videmus in homine quod est unum primum membrum a quo omnia membra, licet diversa maxime sint, dependent . . . Ad hanc similitudinem alias existimavi mundum hunc gubernari a corporibus caelestibus quoniam corpora caelestia sunt sicut cor . . . Ideo talia faciunt diversos motus, tamen omnes tales motus sunt a corde, scilicet caelo.' ('Man is a microcosm, that is a little world, whence we see in man that there is one chief member on which all the members, though they be very different, depend . . . With regard to this likeness, I have considered elsewhere ('alias') that this world is governed by the heavenly bodies since the heavenly bodies are like the heart . . . So such things make different movements, yet all such movements stem from the heart, that is from the heavens.') That *alias* amongst other things refers to the

Apologia, where one reads: 'Dicimus illa superiora non solum concurrere ad irrationabilium effectus, verum et omnium rationabilium . . . omnia haec ab illis corporibus gubernari, ortum accipere, augmentum, diminutionem et occasum.' ('I say that those superior bodies concur with the effects not only of all irrational beings but also of all rational ones . . . all these governed by those bodies and take from them their birth, growth, decline and death.') And still in his commentary to the *Meteore*, referring to the theme of the King (Sun-heart) as the central element in a rigidly hierarchical universe, he imagines himself to be replying to a hypothetical questioner according to whom this kind of universe would be unjust. Pomponazzi's reply is important precisely because it reveals in astrology a general conception of things as a necessary and determinant cosmic order. Astrology in its entirety – including judicial astrology – expresses the rationality of a rigidly graded world, and is, therefore, based as much in natural science as in political thinking. *Natural justice* (and *law*), like *civil justice*, is based on inequality and subordination. 'Dicetis: "si sic, ergo Deus est iniustus." Nego, et dico quod tu es una bestia . . . quoniam . . . non est possibile aliter facere; omnes enim non possunt esse reges et principes. Nam sicut ad hoc quod debeat esse homo vel animal oportet quod sit membrum principale, et non est possibile omnia membra esse equalia in officio, aliter enim non esset homo vel animal; sic, si debet esse mundus, non oportet quod omnes sint equales et ad hoc quod sit civitas non oportet quod sint tot principes. Aliter enim non esset mundus nec civitas et ideo non sequitur iniustitia . . .' ('You will say, "If it is thus, then God is unjust." I deny it, and reply that you are an animal . . . since . . . it is not possible to do otherwise; for not all can be kings and princes. For just as with respect to what a man or animal should be, it is right that there should be a chief member and not every member can be equal in function, since otherwise it would not be a man or an animal; so, if it should be a world, it is not right that all should be equal, and with respect to what a state may be, it is not right that there should be so many princes. For otherwise it would not be a world or a state, and so the injustice does not follow')[13]

Pietro d'Abano and Ibn Ezra, Pomponazzi and Galileo: as one can see, the line of demarcation that humanism tried to trace between astronomy as a rigorous science capable of measuring celestial movements, and astrology as the combination of a conception of the world, of astral cults and prophetic techniques was not only always in danger, but it came to show the untenability of the assumption. Myth revealed itself to be inseparable from reality, rigorous science from transfigurative fantasy, clear reason from turbid magic, religion from superstition, and finally mathematical calculi from the mysticism of numbers. In this sense, the Renaissance controversy about astrology is an exceptional historical experiment. Its events make up the difficult and fascinating story of a lively humanist inspiration, rich in moral force, and faith in reason, which tried to undo the impossible knot, in which were joined irrational instances and memories of archaic astral cults, dreams and chimeras, and which together conflicted with the requirements of high scientific significance. So, often in the same page, refined theories and bold experimentation were placed side by side, and combined with manifestly religious themes, and with echoes of primitive beliefs, while prayer was joined to experimentation. So the poet and the sculptor, the painter and the architect, unconsciously transformed fragments of ancient visions of the universe.

Perhaps the best way of introducing the discussion on

astrology in the Renaissance is to uncover the astrological roots of the theory of rebirth itself: of that which has been characterised as the myth of the *renovatio* (renovation). In other words, whether we look at the ideas and forces which were around from the beginning of the cultural movement which goes under the name of the Renaissance, or whether we reflect on the realisation, which spread quickly from the humanists, of the characteristics of their epoch ('knowledge of the Rebirth' – the consciousness of the Renaissance), we constantly find ourselves confronted with astrological motifs and concepts. They are, in fact, typically 'astrological' concepts whether of 'revolutions' or of 'rebirths': we are dealing, obviously, with cyclical concepts, the alternation of 'sunsets' and 'sunrises', of recurrent periods in astral changes, extended to the human world, to cultures and civilisations, to kingdoms and to religions.

There has been almost too much written on the rhythm of shadow and light, the ages of darkness and rebirth, and so on, in connection with the Renaissance, precisely because it is necessary to repeat it. The Renaissance was in fact awaited, announced and interpreted, as a return to the light, like a new and positive epoch after a period of turmoil. In the fourteenth century the theme of a change of epoch became almost obsessive: *renovatio* (renovation) and *translatio* (transformation) become commonplaces in the anticipation, especially in the West, of decisive events. There is no opportunity here to outline precise historical facts, from the threats of invasions to the crises of the great institutions, which in fact increased fears and hopes, prophecies and utopian dreams. So, on the level of ideas, whether on the side of historical interpretations or on that of ideological elaborations, we find everywhere both in practice and in discussion, the theory of the great 'conjunctions'. Interwoven at times, in the West, with Joachimite prophecy (though the precise mutual influences have still to be thoroughly brought into focus) is the statement of the doctrine set out by al-Kindi and principally expounded by Albumasar, of a close connection between certain celestial phenomena – relative positions of the planets – and the great changes in the history of humanity. Decisive historical crises, such as changes in the leadership of peoples and cultures, the advent or demise of religions, the establishment and the fall of kingdoms and empires: all this was ordered by the movements of the heavenly system. The epochs of man's history could be seen in the skies, in the 'dances' of the stars, in their meetings. The celestial configurations were both signs and causes; in fact they are signs *because* they are also causes, at least if one heeds the masters of divinatory astrology who were most energetically engaged in discussing this very point.[14]

It is clear that one is dealing with a fundamental theme, whether on the theoretical or practical level. On the theoretical level one is dealing with a precise philosophy of history based on a conception of the universe, and characterised by a consistent naturalism and a rigid determinism. On the practical level the acceptance of such a doctrine brings with it the attempt at an exact reading of the heavens to foresee the fates which awaits us, though one was always uncertain whether some kind of escape would be opened to man into the area free from the contingencies which occur under the Moon. The wisest of men is, then, he who reads human history in the stars; and some people hold that, precisely because the knowledgeable astrologer truly interprets the ways of the stars he, and only he, can establish that operative magic which allows one, by making use of the game of the heavenly configurations, to escape their harmful consequences, if they are foreseen in time. Hence the motto of astrologers: 'the wise

man will dominate the stars.' 'Felix, qui secte causas pre-
nosse future / posset venturus per eas in cognitionem, / quis
sibi vivendi modus aptior ad hoc quod / inde mereretur eterne
gaudia vite.' ('Happy the man who can know the causes of
the future mode of life and come through these to knowledge
of what way of living is suitable so that he may thence
deserve the joy of eternal life.')[15] These are verses of the
widely read pseudo-Ovidian poem *De vetula*, which was
in circulation from the thirteenth century, attributed to
Richard de Fournival, often quoted by Roger Bacon, and
which contributed in no small measure to the dissemination
of some of the great astrological theories. This was also
achieved through such works relevant with regard to theory,
as *De causa Dei* by Thomas Bradwardine, an important
vehicle for hermeticism from the second half of the fourteenth century.[16] At the centre of *De vetula*, and in turn the
key to all the astrological themes, was the relationship between microcosm and macrocosm. These are verses which
are worth constantly bearing in mind: 'Mundi partes,
celestis scilicet illa, / hec elementaris, mundo servire minori /
non dedignantur. Mundus minor est homo, cuius / e celo vita
est; et victus ad hiis elementis / sic dictus, quia sit mundi
maioris ad instar / factus.' ('The parts of the universe,
namely that heavenly one and this elemental one, do not
disdain to serve the lesser world. The lesser world is man,
whose life derives from the heavens; and sustained by these
elements thus it was said that he was made in the likeness of
the greater world.') In fact for this reason the heavens, or the
greater world, define the general course of things, and order
the epochs life and death, the demise and the rebirth of the
lower world: 'Ergo necessario nova fient omnia, celum, /
sidera, mundus et hic, et corpora nostra resurgent.' ('Therefore of necessity all things shall be made anew, the heavens,

17

the stars, this world and our bodies shall arise again.')[17] As one can see, the theme of 'newness' – of a new life, a new age, new worlds, new heavens, new earths – which would run so eloquently through the centuries of the Renaissance up till the celebrated writings of Tomaso Campanella and G.B. Vico – was originally nothing more than an astrological common-place.

It is the death and resurrection, therefore, not only of individuals, but also of civilisations in all their aspects. Historians of the Renaissance have often dwelt on the insistent recurrence in the humanists' writings of a reminder of the precariousness of the human fate, right down to the romantic taste for ruins. They often quote famous passages on the destruction of ancient grandeur, on the destroyed monuments of Egypt, Greece and Rome – on the physical death which awaits churches, palaces and castles. So, once again, we are confronted with an 'astrological' theme, which, in order to be understood in its complexity, has to be taken back to the theory of the great conjunctions, or to the theory of the great cosmic cycles, which purport to be at the same time a rational interpretation of what has passed and a prophecy of what is to come; faith and trust in rebirth but also resignation to the inevitable end. One only has to think of the famous lament of Hermes on the fall of Egypt, of its kings, its temples and its gods – a lament which, not by chance, Giordano Bruno was to take up with uncommon eloquence: 'Oh Egypt, oh Egypt! Of your religions there will remain only the fables, still incredible to future generations . . . shadows will be placed before light, death will be judged to be more useful than life.'[18] *The Death of Hermes*, a pseudo-epigraphical text re-introduced by the circles of the Florentine Platonists, was to have a wide circulation for two centuries. The Italian Platonists of the fifteenth century were to insist on the fatal decline of the 'republics' and were to discuss the possibility of a recommencement, of a return to earlier times – of a resurrection of things past, as Machiavelli was to say. Pletho, during his stay at the Florentine Council, had straightaway announced the end of the religious deception of Moses, Christ and Mohamed, and the imminent return of the gods of ancient Greece.[19] Ibn Khaldun, in his *Prolegomena*, almost half a century before, had also described the crisis of Arabian civilisation:[20]

> Buildings erected by Arabs, with very few exceptions, quickly fall into ruins . . . The civilisation of the city then recedes, and its inhabitants decrease in number . . . the architecture of the city reverts to that of villages and hamlets . . . [The city] then gradually decays and falls into complete ruin, if it is thus destined for it. This is how God proceeds with his creatures.

So when Ibn Khaldun was writing, at the end of the fourteenth century, in the East as in the West, the doctrine of the great conjunctions encouraged a lively controversy, and created a doctrinal background to which one does not always give due attention when one discusses the myth of the 'rebirth', of awareness of the *renovatio* and the meaning which contemporaries gave it. At the same time it avoids, at least partially, the tension between hope of extraordinary changes and the fear of the catastrophes which were shaking a great part of the Mediterranean world.

As has been said, the theory of the great conjunctions had been systematically and successfully expounded by Albumasar, whose works were widely read in the Latin and Byzantine middle ages. He lived in Baghdad, and died a centenarian in central Mesopotamia in March 886. Two of his books had a decisive influence in the West from the twelfth century onwards: 'The great introduction to the science of astrology', a systematic treatise in eight books, and another eight books of 'Indications [given] to superior beings' (or to the stars), a title which was rendered in Latin as *De magnis coniunctionibus et annorum revolutionibus aceorum profectionibus.* The *Introductorium maius in astronomiam* or *Liber introductorius major* was translated into Latin twice in the twelfth century by John of Seville and by Herman of Carinthia but only the more condensed yet more elegant version by Herman was printed (in 1489 in Augsburg and in 1506 in Venice). The *De magnis coniunctionibus*, translated by John of Seville, was published in 1489 in Augsburg and in 1515 in Venice.

Lemay's important research has clearly illuminated the contribution which the *Introductorium* made to the entry of Aristotelian physics into twelfth-century Latin thought.[21] But what one must stress next is something else, namely the rigid astral determinism which dominates a book which was widely circulated and read in humanist circles from the fourteenth to the fifteenth century (there is a Florentine manuscript in San Marco which belonged to Cosimo de' Medici and which originated from the famous collection of Filippo di ser Ugolino Pieruzzi).[22] There is no room for man and his initiative: 'Et sicut planete significant possibile atque electionem quod est hominis, similiter significant quod homo non eliget nisi quod significaverint planete.' ('And just as the planets indicate what is possible and the choice man has, similarly they indicate that man will choose only what the planets indicate.') On the other hand the planets, or their inherent 'intelligences', do not choose: 'Planetis autem etsi sunt anime rationales, non eligunt tamen, nec indigent electione.' ('But although the planets have rational minds, yet they do not choose, nor do they need choice.') Celestial determinism is unalterable; all human choice is impossible. In the margin of a manuscript (Paris, Bibliothèque Nationale, lat. 16204) one can read a note, to which Lemay refers: 'Cave, hic sermo durus est'. ('Beware, this discourse is harsh.') It is interesting, perhaps, to remember that the *sermo* (discourse) of a characteristic philosopher of the Renaissance, Pietro Pomponazzi, was to be even more rigid, bitter and disheartened.

However, it is not for this, or not completely for this reason, that the discussion has turned again to Albumasar, but because of a theory which is at the centre of his other work *De magnis coniunctionibus*, which though certainly not original, was brought by his work into the debate in the West. It is important to bear in mind what the *coniunctio*, or *synodos*, is in Ptolemy, who considered it literally as the coupling ('copulatio') of the Sun and the Moon. It was to be rigorously defined by Al-Battani (*Opus astronomicum*, 54): 'Si congressus corporeus in eadem longitudine, latitudine et plaga caeli fit, stellae remanent coniunctae eo usque quo latera ab altera dimidium amborum corporum spatium recedat.' ('If a corporeal conjunction occurs in the same longitude, latitude and zone of the sky, the stars remain conjoined to the extent that they withdraw from each other by half the extent of both bodies.') So, planetary conjunctions in general, and in particular those of Saturn, Jupiter and Mars, are to the world what the horoscope is to man: they are the signs and the causes of great historical events. Ibn Ezra says in *De revolutionibus*: 'Non significant super particularia, immo super communia.' ('They do not give signs about individual events, but about common ones.') As we have said, the succession in the hegemony of religions and kingdoms, of cultures and of customs, is articulated in this way by the sky. It was Ibn Khaldun once again who synthesised the theses of the conjunctionists:[23]

For matters of general importance such as royal authority and dynasties, they use the conjunctions, especially those of the two superior planets . . . Saturn and Jupiter . . . The conjunctions of the two superior planets are divided into great, small and medium. The great conjunction is the meeting of the two superior planets in the same degree of the firmament, which reoccurs after 960 years . . . The great conjunction indicates great events, such as a change in royal authority or dynasties, or a transfer of royal authority from one people to another. The medium conjunction [indicates] the appearance of persons in search of superiority and royal authority; the small conjunction [indicates] the appearance of rebels or propagandists, and the ruin of towns or of their civilisation.

There is no need to continue; except to underline that while Ibn Khaldun was being ironical about the predictions of the conjunctionists, Pierre d'Ailly, cardinal of the Holy Roman Church, at almost the same time, i.e. the beginning of the fifteenth century, did not hesitate to admit the dependence of the birth and reincarnation of Christ on the heavens: 'Sine temeraria assertione, sed cum humili reverentia, dico quod benedicta Christi incarnatio et nativitas . . . per celi et astrorum virtutem.' ('Not with rash assertion but with humble reverence, I say that the blessed incarnation and nativity of Christ occurred through the virtue of the heavens and the stars.') Roger Bacon, as is well known, in the *Opus maius* had fully accepted the so-called horoscope of the religions, repeating Albumasar almost to the letter:[24]

The philosophers want Jove, in his conjunction with the other planets, to signify religions and faith . . . And because there are six planets with which he can come into conjunction, they maintain that there should be six principal religions (*sectas principales*) in the world . . . If he comes into conjunction with Saturn, it means the holy books, that is Judaism, which is older than the others just

as Saturn is the father of the planets . . . If Jupiter comes
into conjunction with Mars it means the Chaldean 'law',
which teaches the worship of fire . . . If it is with the Sun it
means the Egyptian 'law', which means that one worships
the celestial army led by the Sun. If with Venus, it means
the 'law' of the Saracens which is pleasure-loving and
lascivious . . . If it is with Mercury, the Mercurial 'law'
which is Christianity . . . until, at last, the 'law' of the
Moon will come to disturb it and that is the sect of the
Anti-Christ.

Ibn Khaldun ironically said that: '. . . works in poetry and
prose in major verse dealing with forecasts concerning dynasties . . . It is called "predictions" . . . All of these works are
attributed to famous persons. But there is nothing to support
ascribing them to the persons on whose authority they are
transmitted.' In return the conjunctionists in Europe were
enraged. In the very same years in which Ibn Khaldun composed the *Prolegomena*, John of Eschenden, who was connected with the circles of the logicians in Oxford and Merton
College, was dying. However, he composed his *Summa
iudicialis de accidentibus mundi* in the middle of the fourteenth century, in which the great conjunctions themselves
were pointed to as the signs and the causes of the terrible
plague: 'Tanta . . . fuit mortalitas in mundo . . . quod totus
mundus erat turbatus et in pluribus terris relicte erant
civitates et ville deserte et qui remanserunt vivi in eis scilicet
pauci fugerunt ab illis locis relinquentes domos et posses-
siones suas nec audebant homines visitare infirmos nec
mortuos sepelire per timorem infectionis eorum . . . Sed
magna evidentia est quod predicta mortalitas fuit producta
. . . per coniunctiones magnas.' ('There was so much death in
the world . . . that the whole world was agitated and in many
lands cities and towns were left deserted and they who re-
mained alive in them, few indeed, fled from those places

leaving their homes and possessions, nor did men dare visit the sick nor bury the dead for fear of infection from them . . . But there is great evidence that this death was produced by the great conjunctions.')[25]

On the other hand, Nicholas Oresme and Henry of Langenstein (Assia), around the end of the fourteenth century, attacked the *divinatores horoscopios* (diviners of horoscopes) and the *coniunctionistas* (conjunctionists) in works which were destined to contribute many arguments to the debate in the fifteenth century. Indeed, an important fifteenth-century Laurentian manuscript (Ashburnamiano 210) united the anti-astrological writings of Nicholas and Henry in a single collection. It is interesting to note the similarity of emphasis, which Pico had already noticed, between Muslim and Christian polemicists. In 1370 Oresme wrote: 'Multi principes et magnates noxia curiositate solliciti vanis nituntur artibus occulta perquirere et investigare futura.' ('Many princes and magnates, moved by hurtful curiosity, attempt with vain arts to seek out hidden things and to investigate the future.')[26] At almost the same time Ibn Khaldun wrote:

> Rulers and armies who want to know the duration of their own dynasties show the greatest concern for these things and the greatest curiosity in this respect . . . Every nation has had its soothsayers, its astrologers, and its saints, who have spoken about things of this kind. [They have spoken] about a particular royal authority they were expecting, or a dynasty they felt was coming. [They have also spoken] of wars and battles . . . about how long the ruling dynasty would last . . . Things like this are called forecasting.

Astrology and religion, astrology and politics, astrology and propaganda, but also astrology and medicine, and astrology and science: a philosophy of history, a conception of reality, a fatalistic naturalism and an astral cult – astrology was all this and more. The value of the Renaissance debate was to reveal the multiplicity of themes which came together at that time, as it analysed their contrasts and unveiled the insoluble internal contradictions, and all this precisely at the time when the study of the humanists, with its return to the ancient world, seemed to bring new life to the infinite astral divinities.

It is precisely for this reason that one must totally reject the argument, presented as if it were a commonplace, for the possibility of a clear separation, in the Renaissance, between astronomy and astrology (or between divinatory astrology and mathematical astrology). So one gradually comes to refute the simplifications which have accompanied, or alternatively substituted, the idea which was fairly widespread that the rekindling of interest in astrology was solely due to the *studia humanitatis* (study of the humanities), or to the return to the classics.

As we have indicated above, between antiquity and the Middle Ages disparate and complex elements came together in astrology. For this reason no unilateral reduction is worthwhile. So Franz Boll is not persuasive when he states that with the systematisation of Ptolemy the struggle within astrology was substantially settled, because then 'it was not easy for anyone to escape the powerful fascination of such a well-organised system.' Indeed within astrology the most vivid contrasts were coming to light, and not everyone was ready to accept unequivocally the art of the Chaldeans in the heart of which contradictory arguments seemed to be confronting each other. Analogously the attitude of nascent Christianity is anything but simple if on the one hand 'it celebrated the triumph of the love of God over all the powers of the stars and of destiny' and on the other seemed to link the

life of Jesus to astrology, even in the Gospels, from the star of
the Magi to the miracle of the solar eclipse at the death of
Christ. The stars were signs, certainly, and not causes; signs
and messengers from God: but at which point is the distinction agreed upon?

Boll again, on the subject of humanism, asserted that it
'could not fail to reinvigorate the astrological way of thinking since from its beginning it drew, above all, on the literature and the philosophy of late antiquity.' Nothing is more
inaccurate. Indeed it was precisely the vigorous anti-natur-
alistic and anti-scientific aspirations of early humanism
which set alight the anti-astrological debate which went
back to the reasonings of the Holy Fathers. One cannot insist
enough on the inspiration early humanism took from the
Holy Fathers. But Boll is even more debatable when he
attempts to characterise the work of Pico della Mirandola. He
wrote:[27]

> The humanist is the man whose refutations, in an extra-
> ordinarily lucid way, leave a deeper mark than any other
> adversary of astrology; however, nothing would surprise
> anyone who immerses himself in the reading of his works
> today more than the fact that though the humanist con-
> demns the influence of the stars without reservation, he is
> a thinker whose nature is contradictory: he gives more
> weight to Pythagorean mysticism, neoplatonism, cabbal-
> ism and magic than to the aspirations of rigorous and
> rational analysis: a thinker who expresses all the philo-
> sophical tendencies which nourish astrological beliefs, and
> whose deep anxiety to understand the universe as a whole
> would never have made him such an ardent champion
> without the disturbing fascination of Savonarolan pre-
> dictions.

This is hardly the case. Pico felt the need to defend the
free human initiative long before he became a follower of

Savonarola. His attempt to clarify the relationship between man and nature is as old as all his philosophical reflections. Boll does not fully understand the discussion about astrology. Above all he fails to see that in the astrological problem (and in that of magic) is reflected the exasperating central difficulty of the new humanist culture: if human science is to be valid, iron laws of nature are necessary: but if universal and necessary laws of nature exist, how is free and creative human activity possible? If everything is already written in the heavens, what sense has the work of man?

The case of Petrarch is also exemplary in this, being such a constant defender of man's freedom and initiative. However when he wants to represent in *Africa* 'The Palace of Truth' – as he calls it in the *Secretum* – he places a fantastic construction on the yokes of Atlas, all interwoven with astrological signs and similar to the castle Hermes built in Egypt, according to a medieval magical tradition, preserved in a celebrated Arab text on necromancy, the *Picatrix*. In the hermetic text the tower of the castle has on its summit a luminous globe whose lights slowly take on the colour of the planets according to the days of the week. In Petrarch's palace precious stones of various colours symbolise the planets, while 'medio carbunculus ingens / equabat solare iuber largoque tenebras / lumine vincebat: mira virtute putares / hunc proprios formare dies, hunc pellere noctes / solia ad exemplum . . .' ('A great carbuncle, placed / in the mid-point, with splendour like the sun's / effulgence, banished every shadow. / Well you might have deemed its lustre could avail / to generate the day and banish night / true image of our Phoebus', translation cit. in n. 28, bk III, p. 45, lines 125–8). Not only this, but all the various astrological images feature in Petrarch's palace, and are described in minute detail in his refined hexameters: and it is, let us not forget, the abode of Truth. From which, for example, it is worth referring to the rather characteristic representation of Venus:[28]

> Venus,
> and her unseemly source. And it is she
> we next observe, as, new born, she comes forth
> out of the sea, her lowly origin,
> as legend tells. See how, lascivious,
> she rides within the cradling couch, adorned
> with crimson roses while swift flying doves
> provide her escort; mark her company,
> three naked girls, the first averts her face,
> the others outward look with smiling eyes,
> and all have snowy arms entwined in sweet
> reciprocal embraces.

Chapter 2

Astrology and magic: Picatrix

We have emphasised intentionally the theory of the 'great conjunctions' on this subject, even if it is a later doctrine, drawn principally from Arabic astrology, and challenged at times by those same astrologers. Franz Boll described it as menacing and destined to trouble people of both the West and the East with its forecast of great catastrophes; nevertheless, in some of its aspects, for example the so-called 'horoscope of religions', it was full of an uncommon critical power, provoking problems and discussions. Obviously it does not exhaust the field of divinatory astrology, and is only placed after the treatment of 'birth' and 'nativity'. However, it is precisely the theory of the conjunctions which shows clearly that it presupposes a general conception of reality and implies a precise philosophy of history. By incorporating enlightened religions into the train of cosmic events, it subordinates them in some way to the destiny of all things and to the absolute laws of nature on which the rhythms of all cultural events come to depend. Temporal events and geographical movements of civilisations and religions, of hegemonies of men and peoples, are regulated according to the universal course of the cosmos, just as individual and national characteristics depend on climates. As the stars emerge, as they rise and set on the horizon, so the cities, the empires, the churches flourish and decay, grow old and die, and in their turn are born again to a 'new life'. As has been said, the same theme of the *renovatio*, of the *rinascita* is an astrological theme.[1]

From this situation a kind of deep tension comes between the Renaissance humanist's insistency, which opposed the free activity of man to natural determinism, and the concept of a rebirth written in a cyclical course of events, which seems to subordinate every event in human history to celestial movements. This also gave rise to the effort to ensure man's initiative through a work of distinction and importance, which in fact separates within astrology what is a rigorous naturalistic conception from what is possible by individual decisions and choices, without however denying the rights of reason and of science. Petrarch's position is again a good example of this, as he was aware of the consequences of Aristotelian physics, which had been introduced into the West, not by chance, mainly through Albumasar's work. Petrarch realised that astrological determinism ended up by reducing culture to nature, 'civil justice' to 'natural justice' – or rather to the necessity of natural laws. But he also saw, with equal clarity, the close connection with the danger hidden in Aristotelianism, above all in the physics and science of the schools. For this reason in his famous *Invectiva contra eum qui maledixit Italie*, which is a true and real reprimand against Scholasticism in general, and against the Sorbonne in particular, he manages to refute in one fell swoop all of Greek science.[2]

> Cicero [he exclaims] did not write the *Physics*, but he wrote about legislation . . . Cicero did not write the *Physics* but he wrote about . . . old age, friendship, consolation, glory, oratory and on perfect discourse . . . Varro did not write the *Metaphysics* but he wrote 25 books on men and 16 on the

gods . . . He did not write the *Metaphysics* but he wrote about philosophy, poetry, on the Italian language, on the life of the Fathers . . . For we are not Greeks, nor barbarians but Italians and Latins.

Humanity means freedom, the capacity to construct a world for man beyond the boundaries of necessity, to overcome physical causality, dominating it and using it to one's own advantage: to cause culture to rise over nature and not to determine it within the necessary and necessitating orbit of nature. In the seventh letter of the first book of *Seniles*, written to Francesco Bruni, about death, Petrarch denies that the stars could be signs because they are not causes, and he distinguishes the beginning of all things from the totality of things and from the physical universe in general: from the light of the stars comes the light of the light, from the light of the eyes comes the light of the mind. The astrologers 'worship the celestial army, the moon, the sun, the stars from their roof-tops . . . They see the rising and the setting of the stars as the cause of human events', thus confusing different levels of reality – causes with effects.

Petrarch's revolt against astrology became radical: in his work there is a concept of a world which centres around humanity and which opposes not the technique of prognos- tication or science, but another conception of the world which is centred around nature and the eternal physical immutability. So – contrary to what Franz Boll thinks – Petrarch's refutation was to be, in the end, clearly defined, though it is easy to find nuances and distinctions in others' work, even in those close to Petrarch's way of thinking. Take St Bernardino of Siena for example, who was a man of great piety, but who was quick to recognise the validity of astro- logy at least on the physical plane, in the corporal world. Planets and constellations – he preached on the Campo di

Siena in 1427 – govern the body. So one must study the heavens before cutting down a tree or before administering a medicine.[3]

> You will see that when you want to give medicine to an invalid, the doctor says: it is good to give it to him on such a day; and by giving it to him on the day that is safe, it will do him good; and by giving it to him on another day, and not being careful about the days on which you do it, you could do him harm.

So Bernardino believed, through a kind of rigorous division of power, in preserving the stars and the soul:

> The other realm is the spiritual, which is the soul, and this soul is above all corporal things . . . This soul is in height and virtue above the whole of the earth, above the water, above fire, above air, above all things which belong to these elements. The soul is above the realm of the Moon, of Mercury, and Venus, of the Sun, of Mars, of Jupiter, of Saturn and of all the signs which are in them: it is above the 72 constellations.

But the difficulties began when he was presented with the irremediable antagonism between free human choice and physical necessity. Here Bernardino, while he praises the power of free will, seems to want to throw the astrologers' doctrines back in their faces.

> Pray, hate the saying of the pagans if it is true: *Sapiens dominabitur astra* – the wise man will dominate the stars . . . Doctors who know the planets, and the signs and the constellations which govern us, if they have to give a medicine to a sick man, they do so by way of some small thing . . . so that small thing may take away the force from the planet which is passing at that time . . .

What St Bernardino touches on, but without going into it in depth and almost without realising it, is one of the most serious problems within divinatory astrology: that is the relationship between the theoretic moment, or the reading of the heavens, and the operative moment. A problem perhaps which had been more acutely presented by a follower of Petrarch, Coluccio Salutati, who had explicitly confronted the anti-astrological debate more than once. For Salutati too – and he was to say it in prose and in verse – it is easy to identify the irreducible contrast between the two conceptions of the world at the root of the discussion on divinatory astrology: that which underlies astrological determinism, which negates any freedom and hence any humanity; and that implicit in a humanistic culture, which hinges on free human initiative. Salutati's position, however, is neither simple nor straightforward. In July 1378, a few years after Petrarch's death, he wrote: 'Leave free will to human kind; if you try to take it away you will destroy both the human and the divine.' ('Use the stars thus, thus believe in the heavens, that you may leave judgement on the other side with freedom to mankind, because if you try to remove it by proof, you remove the mortal and the divine at once.') These are lines which were actually sent to an astrologer, Jacopo Allegretti of Forli, who had foretold the war between Florence and the Holy See, 'de Martis stelle natura situ influentiaque' ('on the nature, position and influence of Mars's star'). He was also to put them later in the first chapter of the third treatise of his great work *De fato, fortuna et casu*, in which he was also to discuss divinatory astrology and the astrologers (among others Cecco d'Ascoli) showing them 'how much vanity it is', but illustrating, with the ambiguous difficulty of a controversy, the ambiguity of the object of the controversy.[4] If it is in fact useful to know 'the mysteries of the stars' how does one escape heavenly decrees? and how does one obtain knowledge of the entire physical universe, which seems indispensable for

33

a sure prognostication? In 1366, whilst lamenting the death of the astrologer Paolo Dagomari, Salutati was to observe that the rulers of the states ought certainly to investigate the future. But how? Is prediction based on 'study' (*studium*) or on 'natural disposition' (*ingenium*)? Is there any point in talking about scientific research in the field of astrology? If we run through – he went on to observe – the study of the heavens from Ptolemy onwards, we see that the astronomers have made endless mistakes and there are still all kinds of uncertainty about their calculations. King Alfonso claims to have given perfect measurements in his 'tables', but one can immediately see their imprecisions (Alphuns / . . . motus celi ac errantia credidit astra / non erratura tandem ratione dedisse / . . . en magno iam nunc errore notantur / Alphonsi tabule . . .') ('Alfonse . . . believed he had given the movements of the heavens and the wandering stars with a computation which did not stray . . . but now Alfonso's tables are known [to contain] great error.') But even if one achieves full knowledge of the celestial situation, how can individual differences be made to depend on uniform causes? and the different destiny of twins on the same configurations? ('Tell me why the stars dispense such different fates to twins . . . why one rules, but the other serves . . .')[5]

However the most complicated knot of questions emerges where the theoretical moment of understanding fate seems to clash with the hypothesis that there are techniques for escaping fate. Or when, even before that, the fundamental element of the technique of prediction seems to appear to be not only the situation in the sky, but also the complex game of the sentiments and movements of the human soul. It is indeed in the *De fato* that Salutati finds that he has to take account of geomancy at a certain point, and of its relationships with astrology. However, geomancy goes beyond the

simple consideration of astral configurations, and thus beyond the theories of the conjunctions and of birth, and links
itself instead to the doctrines and to the techniques of interrogations and elections, that is questions and choices about
particular events, about the individual cases in life. Not only
this: questions and choices only have meaning in as much as
one looks forward to the possibility of escaping destiny, by
means of an adequate preventative knowledge – in as much
as man is always presented with a choice by means of which
he can avoid a particular unlucky event. The wise man,
indeed, will dominate the stars.

If the configuration of the sky at the moment of birth (or
conception) defines the fate of man; if the conjunctions order
the events of religions and empires throughout the millennia,
so deciding the course of the human collectives, the pro-
cedures of the 'interrogations' and of the 'elections', to which
geomancy is linked, substitute the fatal filiation of man from
the planets with what has been called a kind of elective
filiation. Let us use, and adapt, a Platonic expression – if it is
true that the demon (or the star) chooses man, it must also be
true that man, sometimes seems to be able to choose the
demon (or star).

It is truly through geomancy, even more than through the
general 'interrogations', that very different elements in the
sphere of divinatory astrology emerge, and at the same time
celestial influences and deep psychic reactions become inter-
linked. The signs of the sky can be read, not only in the book
of the stars but also in the reactions which the celestial
influences determine within the individual human being.
Indeed astral influence, registering deep within man, and
moulding him, makes him like a page which reveals the disposition of the stars, if only one knows how to decipher how
much is happening beyond the threshold of the conscious will.[6]

With his usual clarity and brevity, which we often search for in vain in the discussions of the Latins, Ibn Khaldun stresses the gap in this subject between the Arabic astrologers and Ptolemy, who instead aimed at a rigorous rationalisation, and so at an integral mathematical precision in astrology. Ibn Khaldun already saw an ambiguous recall to the psychic unconscious creeping into the technique of the 'interrogations' as well as into geomancy. But it seemed to him that there ought to be astrological 'interrogations' concerned exclusively with the inspection of the sky at a given moment, ignoring any psychical analysis of the questioner, and so basing itself on a purely mathematical reconstruction of the specific situations at a given moment. Ibn Khaldun writes:

> Ptolemy discussed only nativities and conjunctions which, in his opinion, come within the influence of the stars and the positions of the spheres upon the world of the elements. Subsequent astrologers, however, discussed questions (*interrogationes*), in that they attempted to discover the innermost thoughts by attributing them to the various houses of the firmament . . .

Ibn Khaldun denies that the astral influences might determine unconscious psychic movements, where they are translated and faithfully mirrored:

> It should be known that the innermost thoughts concern psychic knowledge, which does not belong to the world of the elements. They do not come within the influence of the stars or the positions of the spheres, nor do (the stars and the positions of the spheres) give any indications with regard to them. The branch of questions (*interrogationes*) has indeed been accepted in astrology as a way of making deductions from the stars and positions of the spheres.

For Ibn Khaldun the technique of the astrological 'interrogations' is very different from the probing of the unconscious, and so too from the forms of clairvoyance which might be verified when the geomancers try to interpret the signs spontaneously traced by the questioner. It is indeed possible that certain geomancers, '. . . attempt to remove (the veil of sense perception) by occupying their senses with the study of combination of figures, they attain intuitive supernatural revelation through complete freedom from sense perception.'[7]

As one can see Ibn Khaldun's exposition and analysis are subtle and penetrating particularly in their emphasis on the play of the unconscious and of spiritual intuitions in some divinatorial techniques, which on the other hand he tends to confine to the level of extraordinary phenomena but not however to the supernatural level (*mirabilia*, things to be wondered at, not *miracula*, miracles). That which escapes him, though it did not escape the Renaissance debaters, is the separation, which is so wide as to be almost a contradiction, between the doctrine of the 'interrogations' (*interrogationes = eroteseis*) as a presupposition of the 'elections' (*electiones = katarchai*), and the theoretical endeavour made by Ptolemy in the doctrine of birth (*genitura*). Birth enchains the individual, and any act, once and for all, at the very beginning (at birth, or perhaps at conception). The stars, the heavens, determine in a second – the first moment, the fatal hour – the whole course of a life: the fate is sealed once and for all, concentrated in a decisive point – the point in which the astral positions discharge the sum of their radiations on the new being coming to life.

So, if at birth the stars choose the destiny of man, so man, through the technique of the 'interrogations', discovers the alternatives still open to him, the intervals of indifference, in which he can invert the process and choose, in his turn, his own star. The *Speculum astronomiae*, disputed in authorship

between Albertus Magnus and Roger Bacon, but probably
written by Albertus, specifies: 'Pars iterum interrogationum
docet judicare de re de qua facta fuit interrogatio cum inten-
tione radicali, utrum scilicet perficiatur, an non? et si sic,
quid sit causa illius, et quando erit hoc? et si non, quid
prohibet?' ('But part of the interrogations teaches one to
make a judgment on the thing concerning which the interrogation was made with radical intention, namely whether it
shall be accomplished or not? And if so, what its cause will be
and when it will be? And if not, what will prevent it?') The
choice will depend on a convergence of matter (*res*) and the
interrogation (*interrogatio*): 'Rursus pars electionum docent
eligere horam laudabilem incipiendi aliquod opus ei cujus
nativitas nota fuerit per convenientiam domini rei cum sig-
nificatore nativitatis ejusdem.' ('Again part of the elections
teaches one to choose a praiseworthy hour to start some task
for someone whose nativity is known through the meeting
and the ruling matter with the sign of his birth.')

All this implies a series of notable variations in the way of
understanding birth, nor is it chance that the *Speculum*
observes that, if the 'births' (*nativitates*) are 'natural things'
(*res naturales*), the 'interrogations' (*interrogationes*) (and
the 'elections') are 'like natural things' (*similes naturalibus*). In fact, the initial influence is not placed and concentrated solely at birth; it is as it were distributed in the
successive moments of life. Man is somehow reborn in every
moment, though the first celestial influence continues to
operate in every moment, but as though in a kind of continual discontinuity. So the questioner, in the very act of the
interrogation, reveals also the secret of his own birth to the
astrologer in the sense that the moment of interrogation can
be considered as being the moment of birth, or more precisely
a new birth. 'Take the interrogation itself in place of birth as

a foundation . . . if the birth is unknown, take his most certain interrogation, since when a man interrogates, he comes then from his birth to the good or evil which his birth indicates.' It is also interesting to note, contrary to Ibn Khaldun's observations, how one can see all the original stimuli of the birth emerging through the unconscious during the interrogation. The interrogator reveals the signs of his destiny in his behaviour, in the way he puts his questions, in his every attitude. A famous astrologer, Haly Albohazen, writes:

> When someone comes to you whose mind you do not know, and you want to know it, first of all let him sit where he wants, at the moment he wants, and then consider how and where he is sitting . . .

On the other hand, when the astrologer identifies more exactly the relationship between the interrogator and the celestial configuration, the possibilities which will allow liberating choices will show themselves much more clearly.[8]

As one can see, and Ibn Khaldun has emphasised it, all this psychological maze had nothing to do with the mathematics of the prophetic astrology of Ptolemy. Ibn Ezra, and Pietro d'Abano following him, said 'Ptolomaeus autem concessit revolutiones et nativitates . . . sed non invenit interrogationes esse veras . . . Doronius tamen asserit fore veras.' ('Ptolemy conceded revolutions and nativities . . . but he did not find that the interrogations were true . . . Doronius (i.e. Dorotheus of Sidon) however asserted that they were true.')[9] One is also dealing, as has already been said, with a fundamental question, and that is the link between the theoretical moment and the practical application of the knowledge of the cosmos, both in the celestial sphere and in the sphere of the elements. Here one approaches, at the same time, the delicate link which connects astrology and active magic ('the practical part of natural science'); here one faces the mass of links between celestial configurations and psychical forces, between the imagination and the emotions, between astral signs and corporal influences. That is to say, one enters the realm of the so-called science of images, of magical ceremonies and talismans. One reads in the *Speculum*: 'Parti autem electionum dixi supponi imaginum scientiam, non quarumcumque sed astronomicarum.' ('I have said that the science of images, not of every kind but of astronomical ones, has, however, replaced part of the elections.') At the centre is Hermes: 'Ex libris quoque Hermetis, est *liber imaginum Mercurii*, in quo sunt multi tractatus, unus de imaginibus Mercurii, alius de characteribus ejus, alius de annulis, et alius de sigillis.' ('Also among the books of Hermes, there is the *Book of Images of Mercury*, in which there are many treatises, one on the images of Mercury, another on his characters, another on rings, and another on seals.') Nor can one separate this aspect of hermeticism from the other 'theological' one, which was destined to be so popular in the second half of the fifteenth century, but which was already creeping in, through the most unsuspected channels, at the end of the fourteenth.[10] On the other hand it is right here, in this mediation of images, which have the task of concentrating the celestial powers and directing them, that the most distant legacies of astral cults emerge. The moment of transition from the mathematical definition of the celestial configuration to the attempt at transforming its consequences, dominating and directing them, is when calculations are substituted by exorcism, sorcery and prayers, whilst celestial bodies and places assume the faces of gods and demons. The position of the man who is born in relation to the sky is no longer rigidly denoted by measurement and numbers: it is seen with joy or with horror, as auspicious or inauspicious, good or evil. The radiations are no longer situated in the spectrum of elementary qualities which are qualitatively variable; they are friendly or hostile aspects of divine spirits. Mars and Venus, the Sun and the Moon, Jupiter and Saturn reassume the attributes of the ancient divinities whose names they bear: every place, every point of the sphere is populated with demons, fabulous animals and living signs. The map of the heavens no longer presents a well-proportioned picture of physically determined bodies in measurable positions and distances, in numbered relationships, with radiations which are either combined or else eliminate each other, which act in different ways according to the angles of incidence or their intensities. A marvellous yet frightening canopy stretches over us, from which demonic beings, good and evil divinities, with their endless retinue, emanate influences of every kind, both fatal and life-giving. Even the 'sweet' Petrarch sings: 'Hec supra horrificis diversa animalia passim / vultibus et variis cernuntur . . . figuris.' ('Above this various animals are seen everywhere with horrifying faces and diverse shapes.') And here, in the world, one must struggle to neutralise, or to divert or transform cosmic radiations, either making them converge and become concentrated if they are good or dispersing and weakening them if they are evil, with the help of stones, of rings, seals and so on. Not only this but one must also exorcise demons and pray to gods; one must imprison them in false and seductive images – one must, in other words, enter the magic circle of the spirits.

As one can see, magic and astrology are always presented as being connected but in two perspectives: one being the general conception of reality and history which aims at the rigour of sciences and techniques: the other is that complex inheritance of ancient beliefs and cults with the suggestion of all kinds of images. Nevertheless the boundaries between the two points of view do not run in straight and clear-cut lines, neither is it always possible, even with the most attentive reflection, to trace strict distinctions between them. Certainly, as medicine became more rigorous as a science, it seemed, as Pico suggested, to dissipate on the one hand the idea of stellar influences, on the other the belief in the effectiveness of magic formulae and talismans. However, the most serious doctors made observations about the cyclical recurrence of critical days, the harmony which periodic phenomena have with the Moon, not to mention the undeniably therapeutic effect of influential formulae working through the imagination and the emotions.

With his usual critical acumen, Ibn Khaldun denounced the mixing of divinatory astrology, magic and superstitious cults:

> These are sciences showing how human souls may become prepared to exercise an influence upon the world of the elements, either without or with the aid of celestial matters. The first kind of sorcery, the second kind is talismans. These sciences are forbidden by the various religious laws, because they are harmful and require [their practitioners] to direct themselves to [beings] other than God, such as stars and other things.

Ibn Khaldun, with a radical rationalism which seems to anticipate the criticisms of Giovanni Pico by almost a century, and in some respects to go beyond him when, finally, he rejects astrology as a whole, reduces magic without a doubt to a mere trick of illusion. Magic is on the one hand a cult of false divinities, and on the other it is imagination without effect. The unavoidable merging of

divinatory astrology and ritual magic inevitably degenerates
into trickery and impiety.[11]

> The person who exercises this kind of influence relies upon
> the powers of imagination . . . He plants among them dif-
> ferent sorts of phantasms, images, and pictures, whichever
> he intends to use. Then, he brings them down to the level of
> the sensual perception of the observers with the help of the
> power of his soul that exercises an influence over that
> [sensual perception]. As a result the [phantasms etc.]
> appear to the observers to exist . . . while, in fact, there
> was nothing of the sort. This is what the philosophers call
> 'prestidigitation' . . . All magical exercise consists of
> directing oneself to the spheres, the stars, the higher worlds
> or to the devils by means of various kinds of veneration and
> worship and submissiveness and humiliation . . . Thus,
> magical exercise is devotion and adoration, directed to
> [beings] other than God . . . Sorcery is unbelief.

In his analysis, Pico was instead to preserve natural magic
and he sought to define its scientific character, that is as an
active science, while on the other hand the theories of Avicenna on the effectiveness of the imagination and the possibilities of obtaining not only illusions but real and marvellous effects through it were to become very popular in the
fifteenth and sixteenth century. '*Quantum faciat fides et
imaginatio*' ('How much faith and imagination can do') –
Pomponazzi was to say – '*abunde patere potest*' ('can be
made abundantly clear'), trying in this way to reduce the
miracles themselves to the sphere of natural effects. Pomponazzi was to make use of Avicenna, but he completely
reversed his theories to a naturalistic meaning; at the same
time he decisively opposed Ficino, who instead would have
accepted 'the good advice' of Avicenna: 'You know that
within nature there are marvels, and that the active superior
forces unite with the passive inferior ones to produce extra-

ordinary things.'[12] Pico, when defending natural magic, was
to speak of unions: the union of the sky with the earth
('Magicam operari non est aliud quam maritare mundum.'
('The practice of magic is nothing other than marrying the
universe.')) A critical spirit such as Galeotto Marzio da
Narni, who was described at the recent 'Colloque inter-
national de Sommières' on *Aspects du libertinisme au XVIe
siècle*, as 'a pioneer of free thought in the fifteenth century',
in defending divinatory astrology from the criticisms of
Averroës praises Avicenna, on the medical and experimental
plane, above all for the use he makes of divination and
magical practices. He wrote in the *De doctrina promiscua*, of
about 1490:

> Averroës criticises things about which he is ignorant, and
> though he wants to explain the writings of Avicenna, he
> does not understand what they say. Avicenna thinks that
> the life of men depends on their birth, according to the
> disposition of the giver of the years (*alchochoden =
> oikodespotes tes gheneseos*) . . . It is therefore the con-
> dition of birth, and not the hands of the doctor which either
> lengthens or shortens life. Manilius correctly said [IV, 16]:
> 'In being born we die and our end depends on our begin-
> ning' (*nascentes morimur finisque ab origine pendit*) . . .
> Those who ignore astrology are only doctors in name and
> not in deed.

And again:[13]

> As Avicenna affirms, the human soul has the power to
> transform things (*vis rerum immutandarum*). In fact, the
> violent longing (*affectus vehementissimus*) in man can
> fulfil whatever he wishes, straightaway, as the magicians
> testify and the Christian faith confirms where it says: 'If
> you have as much faith as a grain of mustard, and you say
> to this mountain move, the mountain will move' . . . But
> whoever wants to know what makes this violent feeling –

faith – work in us, must listen to the words of Galen . . . 'The doctor in whom the sick confide, and in whose hands they put themselves, heals all the more' . . . Avicenna therefore is not wrong in stating . . . that the action of such faith is more effective than all instruments and medicines.

Giovanni Pico della Mirandola wrote in one of his famous nine hundred *Conclusiones*: 'What the magus does with his techniques, nature accomplishes naturally by making man' – that man which, at the same time, he defined as 'the great miracle' (*magnum miraculum*). Man, in other words, in as much as he is *faber* (maker), seems to have a natural vocation for magic. Again in the *Conclusiones* he observed that there does not exist, neither in the heavens nor on earth, any power which the magician cannot unify and realise. Magic, which celebrates the union of the sky and the earth, is for Pico inextricably linked to astrology, even if it is true that the constant force of his reflections was directed towards distinguishing astrology and magic in so far as they are scientific knowledge and the practical applications of the force of nature, from a harmful concept of astrology and of magic as superstitious beliefs in astral divinities and illusory evocations of demonic powers.[14]

They fabricated [he wrote of the cultivators of divinatory astrology and ritual magic] that everyone's fate depends on the stars; and particularly that of princes: sons, life, power, victories, health. They said that, having studied the movement and nature of the stars at length, they saw clearly the future, both happy and sad. They claimed they possessed remedies for warding off foreseen disasters, and the means of making happy events more certain. They stated that if one observed a happy moment, they could make up images similar to celestial natures with special materials, by means of wonderful artificers attracting the qualities of the stars to them and thus making men happy and powerful, and satisfied in their desires whenever they carried with them images made in this way.

The theory of the 'images', on which Ficino dwelt at such length in *De vita*, showing its importance also in the medical field, is justly considered decisive by Pico for the link between divinatory astrology and ritual magic – or the cult of astral divinities and propitiatory techniques. The celestial powers, in fact, come to be caught, and placated or used, by imprisoning them in fictitious material representations, talismans and amulets, capable of absorbing and concentrating astral forces. 'The sages' – one reads in the famous *De pluviis* by al-Kindi – 'have proved through frequent experiment that figures and characters inscribed by man's hand on various materials with a purpose and with due solemnity, observing the place, the time and other circumstances, have the power to move objects.' Such figures, corresponding to celestial 'figures', pick up and reverberate the active radiations of the heavens.[15]

So, this thesis, which is at the centre of the Renaissance debate, is consigned in an almost emblematic way to a work which, for its significance and implications, could be considered parallel to Albumasar's book on the conjunctions in the magical field. That is to say the *Picatrix*, a text well known to Pico and to Ficino, and used by them, but which was also widely read in the fifteenth century in a Latin version, derived from the Arabic through a Spanish mediation. It is not a coincidence that the *Picatrix* is the same book which Ibn Khaldun analyses and discusses when he wants to refute ritual magic and talismans. He does not in fact hesitate to define the *Picatrix* under its title 'The aim of the wise man' as 'the most complete and best written treatise on magic'. Nor is it unimportant that such a cultured thinker as Ibn Khaldun, who died in 1406 and who lived between North Africa and Egypt, should give, at that particular time, such prominence to a work whose influence was only just beginning to be felt in the fifteenth century in the West, whilst in the preceding period the traces of it were scarce and uncertain.[16]

However, given the importance that the book had between the fifteenth and sixteenth century ('the reverend father in the devil Picatrix – said Rabelais – 'rector of the diabolical faculty'[17]); given the link with hermetic literature, the fashion for which was launched by Ficino with such success (Hermes Trismegistus is always present and is remembered with great veneration in the *Picatrix*); given the need to have it constantly to hand, not only as a real source, though obviously not declared as such, but also as a document illustrating a general position and way of thinking: for all these reasons it is fitting to pay it more attention than is usual. In reality the Latin version of the *Picatrix* is as indispensable as the *Corpus Hermeticum* or the writings of Albumasar for understanding a conspicuous part of the production of the Renaissance, including the figurative arts.

The original Arabic version, falsely attributed by the same Ibn Khaldun to Maslama al-Magriti, which is in reality a very mixed compilation, a *summa*, at times a kind of anthology, shows signs of being a book put together 'in the kingdom of Spain' around the middle of the eleventh century between 1047 and 1051. Hellmut Ritter, one of its first scholars, supposed that the Latin version of the *Picatrix* was a corruption of Hippocrates. But he later abandoned the hypothesis, which was nevertheless taken up by Corbin. It seems from the internal evidence that Biqratis (Buqratis)-Picatrix is the name of the compiler himself: *liber*, one reads in the Latin version, *quem sapientissimus philosophus Picatris in ni-*

gromanticis artibus ex quampluribus libris composuit (the
book on the necromantic arts which the most wise philosopher Picatrix compiled from many books). From the Latin
manuscripts it turns out that King Alfonso had the work
translated from Arabic into Spanish in 1256; and from this
came the Latin version, which has never been published, and
of which various manuscripts are known, but all written
relatively late. In 1933 Ritter published a critical edition of
the Arabic text which was then translated into German in
1962 in an accurate version produced by Ritter together with
Martin Plessner. This has made possible a precise comparison
with the Latin version, which is somewhat different, and not
only, as is often said, because of cuts and abbreviations, but
also because of some notable variations. This examination,
so important for placing Ficino's hermeticism in the right
perspective, and more generally, all the hermeticism of the
Renaissance, was made using the Latin manuscript 10272 of
the Bibliothèque Nationale de Paris, written in an elegant
humanist hand of the fifteenth century, and a manuscript of
the Biblioteca Nazionale in Florence, transcribed in 1536, it
has been proved, correcting Thorndike, at Brisighella in
Romagna, land of astrologers. Frances Yates, however, has
used a late manuscript of the seventeenth century for her
studies on Bruno.

Where does the exceptional importance of the *Picatrix*
really lie? Precisely, perhaps, because it puts all the vast
inheritance of ancient and medieval magic and astrology
into, on the one hand, the theoretical neoplatonic picture,
and on the other the hermeticist one. And this in terms which
are surprisingly close to the work of the fifteenth-century
Platonic movement, a closeness which is in fact so marked
that it cannot be pure coincidence. In other words the interest of the *Picatrix* does not end with the iconological con-

tributions already employed by the Warburg Institute: from the history of neoplatonic metaphysics to astrological discussions, from theories of the intellect to magical and alchemical questions, from 'pagan' liturgy to talismans and amulets. *The end of the wise man* of the pseudo-Magriti covers very wide areas of the history of culture. And they are all areas relevant to the scholar of the Renaissance. The work's point of departure is the unity of reality divided into symmetrical and corresponding degrees, planes or worlds: a reality stretched between two poles: the original One, God the source of all existence, and man, the microcosm, who, with his 'science' (*scientia*) brings the dispersion back to its origin, identifying and using their correspondences. Thus the second book of the *Picatrix* opens with an aphorism, the ninth of the *Karpos*, the Ptolemaic *Centiloquium*, one of the basic texts of the astrologers: 'All things in this world obey the celestial forms.' The *Picatrix* comments: 'All sages agree that the planets exercise influence and power over this world . . . from this it follows that the roots of magic are the movements of the planets.' Previously the work had made it clear that the theoretical side of 'science' studies the position of the fixed stars and how they make up the figures and forms of the sky, and in what way their rays dart across the planets. However, whilst the description of celestial figures is certainly interesting, especially the parts concerning talismans and magical rituals, the effective fulcrum of the book is always man as the link between the various planes of reality. Thus the theme of macrocosm–microcosm ('the lesser world is like the greater') crops up time and again and becomes more embellished each time. The scale of being, in fact, is made up of symmetrical and corresponding planes. The exceptional condition of man is that he constitutes, more than a being among beings, a reality apart: a possibility open to all degrees of being, and a possibility which is actualised in the most noble science ('science is something exceedingly noble and elevated'): a science which is therefore based on magic and its work. The picture of man given by the *Picatrix* is not without detail; a picture which is in some ways similar to the hermetic *Asclepius*, and in others similar to the *Oratio* of Pico della Mirandola (who also had the *Picatrix* in his library): [18]

> He is a lesser world similar to the greater world; he is a complete, animated and rational body with a rational spirit . . . And rational means capable of knowledge . . . He has a spherical head and the capacity to judge; he has science and writing; he discovers techniques . . . he laughs and cries . . . he has within him a divine power and possesses the knowledge of justice for governing cities . . . he knows that which is useful and that which is harmful . . . he discovers fine inventions, he performs miracles and makes marvellous images; the forms of the sciences are brought together within him, and he is separated from all other sensible animals, and God has made him the maker and inventor of all science and knowledge, able to explain all its qualities, to accept everything in the world, to understand the treasures within everything with a prophetic spirit . . . Man understands all intelligent forms and everything in this world . . . and they do not understand him; all creatures serve him, yet he is the servant of none; he mimics all other animals with his voice when it pleases him. With his hands he can make images which resemble them; with his words he numbers, narrates and explains their natures and actions . . . With his natural voice man has the capacity to make the sounds of all other animals and he can change their form as he pleases . . . The general form of man is the home of the form of the spirit in general.

The discussion continues rich and forceful. Hermetic man, the 'great miracle' of the *Asclepius*, which made such an impression on the thinkers of the Renaissance, is here the magus, the sage, the master of Heaven and Earth: 'Dico quod homo mundus nominatur, et hoc per comparationem ad maiorem, quasi dicat quod quicquid continetur in maiori mundo, continetur naturaliter in minori.' ('I tell you that man is called a world, and this is by comparison to the greater one, just as one says that whatever is contained in the greater world, is contained naturally in the lesser.') The instrument of human power is indeed science which is knowledge of the heavens and of its apparent and occult forms, on all planes of reality, and, also, mastery of the techniques – from formulae to talismans – with which to act on the forces of the world. The most striking aspect of *Picatrix* is perhaps this exaltation of science and of its progress, or of an increasingly deepening vision of hidden and divided forces and of their possible union. The sage is he who discovers the correspondence and unity in the occult as well as the diversity: 'Ad altiora procedere, discurrendo quousque ad mathematicalem veniamus, in qua virtus completur hominis, et per scientias speculativas est perfectus. Et hoc est bonum quod quaerit homo . . . Et ille qui ad ista attigerit, gaudium, laetitiam et durabilem sapientiam habebit in perpetuum et sine fine' ('to proceed to higher things, by hastening through until we come to mathematics, in which man's virtue is completed and perfected through the speculative sciences. And this is the good which man seeks . . . And he who attains these will have joy, happiness and lasting wisdom for ever and without end'). Conversely, he who is not a scholar and a magus is only a man in name. ('He should not be called a man except in name, form and shape of a man.')

On the other hand this science, which is both astrology and magic, had then to be put into practice through inventions and marvellous machines of every type. There is a singular passage in *Picatrix* where the Latin is faithful to the Arabic which makes one think not only of Roger Bacon but also of Leonardo da Vinci. Whoever possesses science makes *magnalia magna* (very great works) on the technical level, not only walks on the waters and transforms himself into every kind of living being, but he makes the rain stop and start, he causes enemy cities and ships to burn in distant places, ('civitates inimicorum comburere, nec non et naves in loca remota'), and makes ships fly in the sky ('ascendere in aere'). This last marvellous invention is even more striking if one thinks that Fracastoro hints at it again in the dedication to Paul III in the *Homocentricorum . . . liber* ('of that ship which he taught goes up and comes down continually in the middle of the ether').

It is worth mentioning another two 'hermetic' texts of *Picatrix* which were not unknown but whose similarity to the themes of the Renaissance thought seems hard to challenge. The first concerns the ideal city, al-Ašmunain, built by Hermes in eastern Egypt, after he had built a temple of the Sun: the perfect city, structured according to precise astrological standards, after Trismegistus had regulated the course of the Nile in correspondence with the movements of the Moon by means of the appropriate 'images'. It is a quite remarkable text, and one which, in its description of the castle, makes one think of Filarete and Campanella:[19]

> Inside (the city) stands a castle with four gates. On the eastern gate is placed the figure of an Eagle, on the western one that of a Bull, on the southern gate that of a Lion and on the northern one that of a Dog. He introduced the spirits which could speak into the images, and no one could enter the castle without their permission . . . On the top of the castle he had built a tower which was twenty cubits high, on top of which he put a globe whose colour changed every day for seven days. And at the end of the week the first colour returned. So every day the city shone with a different colour.

The other text takes us to the centre of the mystical inspiration of *Picatrix* where it clarifies the notion of 'perfect nature' or as the Latin version says 'complete' nature – 'the hidden secret, that is, which is hidden in the same philosophy'. Hermes said:[20]

> When I wanted to reveal the science of the mystery ('secreta operis mundi') and of the processes of creation, I found a dark cave, full of shadows and winds. I could not discern anything because of the darkness and I could not keep my lamp alight because of the force of the winds. Then a being appeared to me in my sleep whose aspect was one of great beauty. It said to me: take a light and put it in a glass lantern which will protect it from the winds, so that it will shine despite the strength of the wind. Thus it will penetrate into the subterranean room.

We are obviously dealing with a commonplace, but one's thought flies to another text, with a different power, inspiration and meaning, although similar in its images, Leonardo's cave. Here too we find the wind ('the arctic North wind strikes again in its rage'); and then the dark cave and the search for the hidden truth:[21]

> Unable to resist my eager desire and wanting to see the great multitude of the various and strange shapes made by formative nature, and having wandered some distance among gloomy rocks, I came to the entrance of a great cavern, in front of which I stood some time, astonished and unaware of such a thing. Bending my back into an arch I rested my tired hand on my knee and held my right hand over my downcast and contracted eyebrows: often bending first one way and then the other, to see whether I could discover anything inside, and this being forbidden by the deep darkness within, and after having remained there some time, two contrary emotions arose in me, fear and desire – fear of the threatening dark cavern, desire to see whether there were any marvellous thing within it.

Doubtless we are on a different track with Leonardo, far from magicians and astrologers, even if for him man is still a microcosm, and so an integral part of the whole, symmetrical and linked to the whole by infinite and mysterious bonds. None the less the culture which surrounded him, which conditioned him and against which he fought a sometimes equivocal battle, was largely dominated by the inclusion of magic and astrology in the framework of a neoplatonic metaphysics, which characterise *Picatrix*. At one point Leonardo, in his crude polemic against necromancy and alchemy and magic, exclaims: 'O mathematicians, shed light on this error! The spirit has no voice, because where there is a voice there is a body.' *Picatrix* on the other hand, and the work of Ficino, are full of voices without bodies.

In conclusion, the importance of *Picatrix* for bringing certain aspects of the fifteenth century into focus lies in the fact that it foreshadowed to some extent certain tendencies and solutions. Magic and astrology find their justification and foundation there within the speculative framework of neoplatonism. The One-All, the Intellect, the Soul of the World, the souls of the stars and spirits of every kind, theoretically 'found' the theory of influences, and the whole scheme of correspondences which link and unify the cosmos. The unity of a universal life, which flows everywhere and gives life to everything, speculatively justifies the universal sympathy, and the multiplicity of operations which man, an abbreviated image of the cosmos, comes to fulfil. So then the link between the totality, object of metaphysical intuition, and the multiplicity of things and events, in which magic operates, presents itself as something fantastic and arbitrary, the logical consequence of that metaphysical and theological vision. The relationship between neoplatonic metaphysics and practical magic shows a precise symmetry: the magic of incantations is the 'scientific' moment suitable for platonic theology. As the former is in reality a 'poetic' vision of the cosmos, so the latter is a 'rhetorical' technique. If the whole is pervaded by 'souls', those which move the planets are 'spirits' ('It is possible to speak with the spirits of the planets') – as *Picatrix* says and as Ficino was to say. In an animated and consentient universe, connected and working together, in an all-understanding sympathy, one speaks with the stars, the plants, the stones: they pray, they command, they constrain, making more powerful spirits intervene through prayers and appropriate speeches. 'Science' comes to a magical formula, not a mathematical one; its methods and its instruments are incantations, talismans, amulets, not machines. The word, the *verbum*, the speech, of which *Picatrix* speaks so much, is the word which rises to the stars or to the stellar divinities or reaches the 'spirits' of things: *quia verbum in se habet nigromantie virtutem* (because the word contains in itself the power of necromancy). As the Arab text says, 'speech is the most beautiful kind of theoretical magic.'

Chapter 3

Neoplatonism and hermeticism

In 1439 the Council for Church Unity moved from Ferrara to Florence: undoubtedly this was important not only on the religious level but also on the political one, and above all on the cultural one. The meeting of the most representative figures of the Christian, Greek and Oriental world with those of the Latin world was an exceptional occasion, and its implications have never been adequately assessed by historians. Doctrines and beliefs confronted each other, books poured in, there were animated discussions, information spread, personal contacts were widened. The passage of the inheritance of Greek thought into Italy, which was to be symbolised and sealed in the gift of Bessarion's library to Venice, came to its culmination in the Florentine Council.

However, when the Greeks defended the originality of the Eastern tradition to the Latins, they unwittingly contributed to the crisis of the mature principles of Western scholasticism.[1]

> The representatives of the Eastern church felt that Aristotle's place in Latin theology (on the guidelines set by Albertus Magnus and Thomas Aquinas), together with Western theologians' use at that time of Aristotelian metaphysical terminology and the intellectual nature of this theology, even in a humanist formulation was an inappropriate intrusion by worldly science into that theology

which is the science of God . . . Even if men like Bessarion
and Mark of Ephesus were perfectly entitled to use all the
scholastic resources of reasoning, the Greeks were of the
opinion that theology had nothing to do with either Aristotle or with the syllogisms. They were more scandalised
than convinced by the dialectical arsenal which the Latins
used to support their own theories.

It was the neoplatonic tradition in general which came to
re-emerge with force in the Greek fathers' thinking, even in
its more daring forms, in what was at times a rather dis-
concerting revival of Hellenism. So one was not only dealing
with an enrichment of knowledge and commentary on Aristotle, through a return to the vitality and rigour of the
original texts, nor was one simply dealing with the integration of Aristotelianism and Platonism, and with a greater
understanding of all the riches of Arabic thought. One had
above all a rediscovery of the Hellenistic age, when all types
of Eastern influences had come together in Greek culture.
Indeed, we see in this situation the singular encounter between the magical and astrological doctrines of the Latin
Middle Ages, whose ancient heritage had filtered down via
the Islamic world, and the Hellenistic positions, which had
been rediscovered in the Greek sources. A confrontation of a
great wealth of theories resulted, sometimes moving towards
an attempt at new syntheses, at others resulting in crises and
radical criticisms. One thing, however, is striking: the Greek
divinities returned to Florence at the very moment when the
Christian world was trying to reunite itself in the face of the
threat from the Turks.[2] Paradoxically it seemed that the
reunification of men had to be found, not in the enlightened
religions, but by going back to the principles in which the
later Greek philosophers had seen the symbols of the supreme
and ineffable divine unity.

It was in that atmosphere that the most serious participant at the Council, George Gemistus Pletho, the restorer of the cult of the pagan gods at Mistra, announced, whilst discussing with his Florentine friends, the imminent end of Judaism, Christianity and Islam, and the advent of the conversion of men to the religion of truth. His implacable adversary George of Trebizond was to write:[3]

> I myself heard him in Florence when he said that within a few years the whole world would have one and the same religion, one mind, one soul, one sermon. And when I asked him if it would be the faith of Christ or that of Mohamed, he replied: neither of these, but another faith which is not so different from that of the gentiles. I was offended by these words, and have always hated him; I have had a horror of him as of a poisonous snake, and I could not look at or listen to him any more. I heard, however, from some Greeks who had fled here from the Peloponnese, that before dying, almost thirty years ago now, he had publicly stated that, quite soon after his death, Mohamed and Christ would be forgotten, and that absolute truth would flower again throughout the whole universe.

As is well known, Pletho was thinking of the resurrection of the Hellenistic divinities, of the cult of Zeus, of Apollo, of the Sun and of the stars. In one of the fragments of the *Peri nomon* saved from destruction and from the persecution of Scholarios, one can read, amongst other things, some very significant prayers:[4]

> King Apollo, you who rule and govern all things in their identity, you who unify all beings, you who harmonise this vast universe which is so varied and manifold . . . O Sun, lord of our heaven, look favourably upon us; and you too, O Moon, venerable goddess, look favourably upon us; and you, the bringer of light (*Venus*), and you Stilbon (*Mercury*), both faithful companions of the resplendent Sun,

and you, Phaenon, Phaethon, Pyrois (*Saturn, Jupiter* and *Mars*), who all obey the Sun your king, who help him as is fit in the government of human matters, we celebrate you as our radiant protectors, along with the other stars which a divine providence has thrown into space.

However, one must not be deceived by the many names of the gods. There is only one God for Pletho, the supreme god whose law is absolute and unchangeable: it is the destiny, the *heimarmene*, which nothing escapes. 'Everything is subject to a law . . . All events are established by eternity, placed in the best order possible under the authority of Zeus, the unique and supreme master of all. Zeus alone among all other beings knows no limits, because nothing can limit him . . .' Nothing can escape his decrees or his foresight, nor that of the superior beings which are his ministers; and knowledge of the future cannot affect necessity. Even those who know, know 'the decrees of a necessary and inevitable Destiny . . . Nor is there any way of escaping, of evading that which Zeus has decided for eternity, and which Destiny has fixed' for ever.[5]

This is the Platonism of Mistra, which was reintroduced into Florence after the Council through the initiative of Cosimo de' Medici. As Theodore Gaza, who joined with Bessarion in fighting George of Trebizond's accusations, suggested, it was a Platonism which was reminiscent above all of Celsus and the Emperor Julian.[6] Naturally Pletho liked to refer to the philosophy of the 'Chaldean Oracles'; undoubtedly he took part in the success enjoyed by Julian's works, and especially his oration to the Sun, which became a text particularly dear in Florentine circles.[7]

However, Pletho's position is important at the beginning of the 1440s, as it had such far-reaching consequences. His prophecy on the end of religions, his enthusiastic welcome to pagan divinities, his appeal to the celestial gods, his rigid determinism, immutable destiny, the chain of all reality: all this constitutes a very singular kind of Platonism, of a materialistic and atheistic nature (Scholarios accused him of atheism). The eternal universe, where everything is subject to destiny (*heimarmene*), is, to use the words of Gemistus himself, 'a marvellous whole, whose state will remain unchangeable for eternity, and for ever in the form impressed on it in the beginning.' The future leaves no mark on existence; the cyclical changes constitute the periods which are always the same in the eternal round of life. This applies to the rhythms in religions and the changes in kingdoms, and even the repetitions of names for the same events: from this follows that there will be more than one Dionysus, more than one Hercules. 'The periods of time bring with them, and will always do so, identical lives and identical actions at fixed points in time, so that nothing ever happens which is truly "new", and nothing happens which has not already happened, and which will not happen again some day.'

Pletho was at the same time both a great thinker and a great reformer. His interpretation of Platonism and Hellenism found its conclusion in a rationalism which exploited the scientific possibilities implicit in astrology to the full. His Zeus, his One-All, his heavens, his destiny (*heimarmene*), carried the consequences of a natural law, which necessitates and links everything together, to their logical conclusions, where everything can be foreseen and is predictable because everything is preordained: where religions, revelations, prophets, apostles and saints are brought back to the absolute plane of reality. There is no doubt that such a conception was irreconcilable with every positive religion; it is not surprising that it should be attacked and persecuted in the East and the West. What is most important in all this is that Pletho himself opened the way to a series of recoveries, however reductive, of great significance: from the praise of the Greek gods to the solar cult, from the 'Chaldean Oracles' to Emperor Julian, from Zoroaster to the 'Mysteries of the Egyptians' of Iamblichus. And it is his work which puts forward the puzzle of the ambiguity of Platonism: a Plato who is the father of every heresy and impiety, and a pious Plato in the dress of an Attic Moses: the Plato who is detested by George of Trebizond as a materialist, an atheist and immoral; the Plato who is exalted by Ficino as the initiator and great master of the devout philosophy (*pia philosophia*). It is the same ambiguity which one finds in the Platonists' discussion about astrology, and which implies two different ways of approaching and interpreting it: one of which, like Pletho, is conceptual and mathematical and reduces the heavenly intelligences and the souls of things to necessary principles of rationality inherent in the picture of an absolute, completely predetermined. The other instead accentuates the personality of the divine and underlines the free individuality of souls, and gives life and humanity to everything, and is expressed in terms which are fantastic and emotive, imaginative and poetic. In the first case one risks losing human initiative and freedom; in the second the trap is the destruction of rationality and a nature which is regulated by laws. A continual tension emerges from this in the oscillations of the thinkers, in the variation of positions, in the changes of the controversy's objects and of the very interpretations which one gives of astrology; an ambiguity which is so deep that it is useless to think it can be resolved by the commonplace of the oppositions between astrology and magic.

An example of this, and of particular relevance, is the work of Marsilio Ficino. This has often been examined and discussed, but with regard to astrology has never been adequately looked at in all its fluctuations and variations. Thorndike strongly insists on the speculative weakness of Ficino in a chapter of his great *History of Magic and Experimental Science*. He deliberately entitles the chapter 'Ficino the Philosophaster', taking up the disparaging term 'philosophaster' from Vives, who had written, quite unjustly: 'He wrote letters that he might discuss Platonic questions with unattractive and laboured speech.'[8] An elegant writer, Ficino, in the letters, indulged heavily in stories and testimonies which could easily confirm an inclination on his part to accept, not only astrological themes, but more generally exceptional and out-of-the-ordinary experiences. It is certain that he agreed with magical and astrological practices; but it is also clear that his standpoint was not consistent. Paul Oskar Kristeller, who was such a careful and detailed analyser of Ficino's work, and the praiseworthy editor of the unfinished *Disputatio contra iudicium astrologorum* written in 1477, observed fairly how Ficino's position was 'ambiguous and full of contradictions'.[9] He recalls that in the *Disputatio*:

> He attacked astrology with a number of arguments, and in 1486 he inserted part of these arguments almost literally into his commentary on Plotinus. But in the third book of his *De vita*, written in 1489 and originally intended as a chapter of the same commentary on Plotinus, he uses astrology in a positive way for the purposes of medicine. Finally in 1494, when Pico wrote his huge work against astrology, Ficino announced his agreement in a letter to Poliziano and then tried to make his previous statements in the *De vita* seem consistent with his (and Pico's) view. However, his justification was somewhat artificial and was received with scepticism by Poliziano. In reality Ficino's own practice during his whole lifetime, especially in his later period, shows that he was not at all opposed to astrology. (tr. cit. in n.9, p.310f.)

So Kristeller, who wisely adds how fruitless it is to insist on the weaknesses and incoherences, says that instead one must examine more closely that which could show its eventual developments and depths: a rigorously diachronic analysis in fact which no one has done to date – and which is not easy to do – but which would certainly be more useful than the severe criticisms of Thorndike, or Marcel's favourable treatment of what are often in Ficino only baroque affectations of style and argument. Two things above all should not be forgotten: firstly, the motives of prudence which sometimes helped to make an argument deliberately obscure; secondly, as has already been hinted at, the huge diversity – contrasts even – between the themes and theories within astrology and magic themselves, and the difficulty in making strict distinctions between them.

Furthermore, one must not overlook Ficino's study of medicine, nor his youthful interest in perspective, in the theory of vision, in 'flat and concave mirrors', in *physiognomia* (about which he had written); it is also worth pointing out that it is precisely towards medicine that Ficino, even in his later years, was to be more energetic in justifying the scientific validity of astrology. 'If you value life' – he was to write in 1489 – 'you will take medicines approved by the heavens. Confirmed by a certain heavenly support (*caelesti quodam adminiculo confirmatas*).' Experience teaches us – 'I have learned from long and frequent experience' ('*frequenti iamdiu experientia compertum habeo*') – that there is the same difference between a remedy chosen 'without the help of astrology' ('*absque delectu astrologico*') and one that is advised by the stars, as between water and wine. Precisely because he took advantage of astrology, he was able to bring a child to life – 'as it were returned to life rather than saved' ('*quasi vitae redditus potius quam servatus*') which had been born after only eight months.

As one can see, the young son of the doctor Diotifeci d'Agnolo di Giusto started with precise medical and scientific interests and never lost them: both in his taste for the language and the methods of geometric optics, and for medicine. In the dedication to *De vita*, addressed to Lorenzo de' Medici, Marsilio, in his role of both jester and courtier, was to insist that he was continuing his own medical vocation and played on the theme of his conversion from the medicine of the body to that of the soul, from Galen to Plato:

> I have had two fathers: *Ficinium Medicum* (Ficino the Medic) and *Cosmum Medicem* (Cosimo de' Medici). From the one I was born and from the other reborn. The first put me in the care of Galen, the doctor and follower of Plato, the second dedicated me to the divine Plato himself. In fact, both have made medicine my destiny. If Galen is the doctor of the body, then Plato is the doctor of the soul.

It is significant that these words are found in the preface to *De vita*, a work which is so strongly astrological, and in a context which underlines the parallel between *De vita* and the *Theologia platonica*: soul and body, medicine of the soul and medicine of the body: 'after those on the soul, these . . . books on the body'.

Medicine, geometric optics, physiognomy, and then Lucretius's poem: these were Ficino's starting points, which were later transformed but never rejected. His first important work as a translator was the *Corpus Hermeticum* which he finished in April 1463 for Cosimo il Vecchio. This was made from a manuscript brought by a monk called Leonardo di Pistoia from Macedonia to Italy and passed on by Poliziano ('recently brought to Italy through the diligence of the learned and honourable monk Leonardo di Pistoia').

One cannot say enough about the enormous importance

and influence of Ficino's hermetic translation. Equally, the area in which the hermetic fashion exploded in such a macroscopic way has not been sufficiently clarified: an area of curiosity and expectancy, encouraged by the quotations of the Fathers, and especially those of Lactantius and Augustine, and even more so those of the *Asclepius* and of the magico-astrological texts circulating under the authorship of Hermes, which were widely used by eminent theologians. Think, for example, of Thomas Bradwardine, famous for his work on proportions, whose great work *De causa Dei* had an immediate circulation in Florence in the middle of the fourteenth century, even amongst the teachers at the university.[10]

The hermetic texts were a constant point of reference for Ficino, a privileged testimony of the ancient theology *(prisca theologia)*, a wonderful document which shows hidden mysteries *(arcana mysteria)*, and which was rightly placed by Lactantius amongst the Sibyls and the Prophets *(inter Sybililas et Prophetas)*. So it is precisely from this point of view that he found the metaphysical and theological proof and foundation of astrology and magic. Frances Yates is right in observing that the third book of *De vita*, full of magic, is an extensive exegesis of Hermes (of the *Asclepius*) rather than a commentary on Plotinus. One can go further: Ficino constantly echoes and takes up Trismegistus.[11] Astrology had been put in a context in his writings which seemed to him to be completely in keeping with not only Christian tradition, but also his vision of man, his dignity and his central position in the cosmos. On the other hand, every act, every power, every instant of life, depends on the stars, and through the stars on the Sun. In the fifth treatise it is said that:[12]

> If you, therefore, want to see God, consider the Sun, consider the path of the Moon, consider the order of the stars.

> Who is it that keeps this order? . . . The Sun, the highest god
> amongst the gods of the heavens, to whom all the other
> celestial gods give way like to a king and a master, yes, the
> Sun with its immensity, he who is greater than the earth
> and the sea, consents to have stars of the smallest mass
> above him which fulfil their own revolution.

The influence of the Sun and the stars, their influxes and
their radiations, and all the forces which rain from the sky on
man and define his fate, are demons, or forces, because the
essence of a demon is force (*daimonos gar usia energheia*).
Ficino was able to find a clear interpretation of some of the
fundamental points of astrology in the sixteenth treatise:

> The chorus or, better still, the choruses of the demons, have
> been positioned, by the orders of the Sun: they are in fact
> numerous and different, positioned by the command of the
> 'squires' [*plinthis*] of the stars, a demon for each star. Being
> so placed, they serve each star, be they good or bad, accord-
> ing to their nature, or according to their energy – the
> demons' essence, in fact, is being energy (*energheia*); there
> are also some mixtures of good and bad.

Here it is not difficult to recognise, in the squadrons of the
demons, an allusion to the thirty-six Decans.

The Hermetic text continues:

> All these demons have received, in some way or other, full
> power from destiny over terrestrial events and over the
> disorders which happen on earth, and they provoke all
> kinds of disturbance for cities and peoples throughout the
> universe, and in particular for each individual . . . In fact
> when one of us is born, and is given life, we are taken into
> the care of the demons in the precise moment [*stigmè*] of
> birth – the demons, that is to say, that have been positioned
> by the orders of each of the stars. The demons mutually
> replace each other from moment to moment; they do not
> always work in the same way, but serve according to their
> turn.

Ministers of the stars and the heavens, they realise the energy
emitted by the celestial bodies in forces or physical radiations
(*physeis, energheia, vires mundanae*) and so personify the
cosmic dynamism. Festugière has very clearly summarised
the position of the hermetic text: 'All sublunary beings are
under the influence of forces emitted by the stars, which are
incorporeal in themselves, but dwell in bodies, and agents
only through the intermediary of bodies. The forces . . .
influence all beings, animate or inanimate.' As a text preserved by Stobaeus says, 'men are subject to Destiny by reason
of the forces at work in their birth.'[13]

So, Ficino, though with time he drew from new sources,
and so enriched his own point of view, fundamentally re-
mained faithful to this basic picture which we will find again
substantially unchanged in 1489, in the *De vita coelitus comparanda*, his most characteristic work on the subject.

How does one explain then the *Disputatio contra iudicium
astrologorum*, written in 1477, which was unfinished and
unedited, but many parts of which were incorporated in the
Theologia platonica, and some of whose arguments were
taken up again in the commentary on Plotinus, written in
1486? The answer is not easy, nor can one keep the coherence
of a linear development. Without a doubt, Ficino always
tends to distinguish the plane of the intelligence and of the
soul from that of matter and of the body, and to subtract the
former from the determination of the latter. Nor is he far from
his Hermes in this, where one reads the peremptory statement
that, 'when the reasonable part of the soul escapes from the
sovereignty of the demons, it remains stable and is ready to
become the receptacle of God.' However, both in the *Disputatio* and elsewhere, one finds a series of concise arguments
which tend to attack the whole of divinatory astrology,
destroying it down to its roots, often outlining a kind of

sketch of Pico's work. One cannot help but be struck by the texts published by Kristeller: the astrologers do not explain causes; their work is not ordered; they are equivocal on the theory of the interrogations; they are wrong in attributing an influence to the positions of the planets, in the doctrine of the 'houses', in the divisions of the heavens, their properties, and aspects, in the exaltations, and so on. Side by side with the defence of divine providence and human liberty is an insistent and detailed scrutiny of the various astrological theories. This examination unites the attempt at a rigorous scientific analysis with the objections of practice and the banal criticisms of the time. On the other hand it is also true that Ficino never carried his anti-astrological censure to its conclusion; that he left aside the most bitter and often conventional objections in his published works; that he did not hide uncertainties and ambiguities; that, above all, he showed that he wanted to fight the materialistic and atheist issues in astrology more than astral determinism.[14] He did not want the stars, among the different planes of reality, by deciding destiny inasmuch as they are celestial bodies, to assume a hegemony and thereby assure themselves priority on the corporeal and material plane. He deliberately puts the attacks on the astrologers with the criticisms of Epicurus and Lucretius, who had been the tempters of his youth, in the *Theologia platonica*. If human souls and intelligences are determined, they are determined by the intelligences and souls of the stars, and through immaterial intermediaries of the same kind; bodies, even subtle ones, determine only other bodies. On the one hand Ficino insisted, almost to the point of exasperation, on the differentiated unity of everything, on its gradation, on its extremely indirect articulation, on the intermediary links; on the other hand he strongly defended the distinction of the planes: 'no one dares say that the minds

of men are moved by the minds of celestial beings through the
sky, as if they were their instrument or intermediary. Mind
comes together with mind rather than with any other body;
and it is because of this that the sky cannot intervene between the minds on high and our own.' But the various planes
or levels in the articulated unity of the whole correspond to
each other in parallel, so that one is the sign and symbol of
the other. The divine movements of the heavens indicate
their intentions, and announce the future by using the
bodies, figures and movements of the stars (*celestibus corporibus et motibus*), as if they were signs and gestures. The
celestial configurations are like the letters in a book which
explain the divine concepts ('the notions of divine beings are
made clear by the disposition of the heavens, as if through
letters'); the decrees of the intelligences are shown through
the stars, 'through signs rather than causes' (*per signa potius
quam per causas*).[15] And astrologers can sometimes read
these signs. Ficino summarised his divine Plato with true
feeling by drawing up a map of the universe which was
worthy of being placed next to the works of the painters of the
time.[16]

> In all the spheres there are rational souls, ordered by
> degrees according to their rank. But Plato called Jove the
> unique soul of the whole mechanism, and the twelve souls
> of the twelve spheres he called the twelve gods who follow
> Jove. Similarly he placed souls which had a share in intel-
> ligence in the purest parts of the spheres, that is the stars
> and the planets, which he also called gods. In the fiery
> regions he placed demons and heroes of fire. In those of the
> clear air, aerial spirits; in those of the dark air, demons and
> aquatic heroes. Finally he joined together intelligences to
> the purest parts of the earth which, as they inhabit the soil
> (*humus*), are called men (*homines*). At times demons and
> heroes are also put on the earth; nor did Plato only place

heroes and demons under the Moon, but he also put them in great throngs in the heavens beyond the stars. But in all the spheres he placed, as well as the prevailing demons and gods, individual souls, both demonic and heroic and like- wise human ones . . . There are as many heroes, demons and souls massed there as there are stars to which they are subject. Under Saturn the saturnian; under Jupiter the jovial; under Mars the martian, and so on . . . He believes that all is part of a whole, but on the earth in a terrestrial way (*modo terreno*), in the water in an aquatic one and similarly in the air and in fire. So it is in the heavens according to celestial nature, on the Moon according to lunar nature, and in other spheres analogously, so that each sphere is a complete world in its own way and accord- ing to its own nature.

Ficino made this vision his own, toning it down but also complicating it, of a world crowded with souls, with masses of souls, of souls which join together – which irradiate each other; they are living and intelligent chains:

All the intelligences, be they those of the highest rank and superior to the souls, or be they inferior and part of the souls, are so interconnected that, beginning with God who is their head, they proceed in a long and uninterrupted chain, and all the superior ones shed their rays down on the inferior ones.

This is the order of providence which gives life to the corporal order through the mediation of the 'idol' (*idolo*) 'that is the image of the rational soul' in which there are 'the seeds of all the movements and the qualities which the soul develops in the body'. And then there is nature or rather an *affectio sive complexio efficax atque vitalis . . . quasi quoddam vestigium animae in corpore sive umbra* (powerful and vital disposition or combination . . . like some trace or shadow of soul in the body). It is a breaking up, but also a weakening, of planes of being, of corresponding series, of different but parallel orders, and at the same time an integration: *connexio et mutua scintillarum infusio* (union and mutual intermingling of sparks). They also have infinite resonances: 'If one strikes one of two equally taut chords of a lyre, the other vibrates with it.' Everything, at the heart of being, is linked to everything else in a continuous bond (*per continua ligamenta*). Using a fire image, Ficino describes the condition of man at the heart of the universe in the thirteenth book of *Theologia*:[17]

> We are therefore tied to the machine of the whole (*toti machinae*) as though with three ropes, to the intelligences with intelligence, to the 'idols' with the 'idol', to natures with nature, in the same way that the foetus is linked in the womb to the whole body of the mother by unbroken ties. So too the foetus perceives with its soul, its body and its 'spirit' the 'passions' of the mother's soul, body and spirit.
>
> The soul is above destiny by its intelligence, in the order of providence it imitates the superior realities and governs the inferior ones with them. Almost taking part in providence, in fact, it guides itself, the home, the city, the arts and the animals by the divine model. Through the 'idol' it is similarly within the order of fate but not subject to fate. The 'idol' of our soul in fact, by its nature, co-operates with the superior 'idols' to shape and move the body. By nature the body is subject to fate; the soul moves the body in fate by its nature; intelligence is above fate in providence; the 'idol' is in fate, above nature; nature is below fate and is above the body. This is the position of the soul in the order of providence, of fate and of nature not only passively but actively.

As one can see, if Ficino denies the dependence of the soul on bodies and hence on the stars, so populating each body, and above all the sky, with souls, he restores the link of the soul with the soul of the star and with all astral souls. 'Do not

increase destiny,' he repeats with the *Chaldean Oracles* and
with Pletho; 'do not subjugate your intelligence to the body
of Heaven; it is enough that the intelligence depends on the
intelligence of the heavens.'[18] The influences remain, on the
various levels – the umbilical cord which links us to the life
of the whole remains, on the level of nature: 'In conclusion,
we are motivated by the dispositions which descend to us
from the universal natures in a long chain, through the
intermediary of our nature [*longo ordine a naturis univers-
alibus*] and we are completely unaware of them because they
urge us on from within.'

On these bases, and with a fundamental coherence, is
founded the magico-astrological position taken up in the
third book of *De vita*, the *De vita coelitus comparanda*, to
which the well-known research of Warburg, Saxl and Panofsky, Klibansky, Chastel, Walker, and Yates has drawn attention.[19] Ficino certainly lays the emphasis on ancient orient-
ations in his work of 1489: but he remains faithful besides the
usual hermeticism, to the thematic substance of the *Theologia platonica*, with the theory of universal animation (and
therefore the harmony of the world), of the soul of the stars,
of demons, of the *spiritus* as an intermediary, of the *idolum*. It
should be emphasised that all these doctrines are not con-
torted and obscure, as they seemed to Frances Yates, but are
in fact very clear, and are succinctly summed up by André
Chastel with regard to *De vita*:[20]

> The universe appears as a gigantic organism in perennial
> vibration because the stars are the origin of the active
> forces in insensible matter, in plants and also in animals.
> Under the direct influence of Alexandrian science, Ficino
> gave a powerful description of the spiritual unity of the
> world under the rain of planetary influences in *De vita*,
> with the correspondences and harmonious coincidences
> which result from it everywhere.

It is indeed the soul – the soul of the world, the soul of man, the souls of all living things (and everything is living) – which is the universal mediator, present everywhere, because 'there is nothing in the living world so deformed that it does not have a soul.' By mediating between the divine intellect and corporal matter, the soul of the world gathers as many seminal intelligences (*rationes seminales*) within itself, as there are *idee* in the divine mind, and reflects them and moulds them as *species* in matter. The soul of the world is the point of intersection of the stellar plane with its rays, its demons, and the meeting place between seminal intelligences for generation (*rationes seminales ad generandum*) and exemplary intelligences for learning (*rationes exemplares ad cognoscendum*). The sky is populated with figures beyond the stars too, and each figure is subdivided into still more figures, corresponding to all the *species* and the properties of the *species* of the inferior world. This is not the place to follow Ficino in his efforts to define the structures of each of the planes of reality, and their reciprocal correspondences and their intrinsic natures, and the way they react to each other through the central mediating activity of the soul. But certainly all the difficulties in his thought are diminished if one grasps the point of the union: what he in fact calls the 'concord of the world' (*concordia mundi*), and which is expressed as the refraction, slowly moving on different planes, of that living unity which is the cosmos, in which each individualisation in turn is the synthesis of all the others. It is like an endless game of mirrors, a succession of images and shadows of images; above the perfect forms of the ideas, below the lessening of planetary influences. And all are 'formal' manifestations of the one living heart of the universe, different signs of that unique living reality which, in its turn, is the same infinite refraction of life. So, the total resumption of astrology does not contrast with liberty, because in the conformity of the variations of things with the stars, no constriction on the part of the stars results, but only a correspondence which expresses a deeper unitary rhythm. 'All the species and properties of inferior things are contained in the stars, in the figures, in the parts, in the properties.'

The *De vita coelitus comparanda* is indeed what Ficino promises when he states: 'I do not so much recommend as report' ('*non tam probo quam narro*'): a demonstration that the whole of astrology is nothing other than the translation of reality into celestial language, an illustrated projection of the whole, in which the fantastic figures of the imagination transcribe the movements of the psyche, the stirring of the affections, the processes of the generations, the chains of concepts. To know how to read all those languages, from the colours of the stones as from astral figures, helps one to understand even better the life of the world.[21]

> The life of the world, present everywhere, propagates itself in the grasses and in the trees, almost as if it were the hair and fur on its body; and then in the stones and in the metals which are almost like its teeth and bones . . . And this common life blossoms still more above the earth in the more ethereal bodies which are nearer the soul. Water, air, and fire have within themselves living beings and they move themselves through its inner energy. This life heats and moves the air and fire more than earth and water. It gives life to the greatest extent to the celestial bodies which are like the head, heart, and the eyes of the world. Finally it diffuses its rays, which are not only visible but can also see, throughout the world through the stars which act as its eyes.

This is how every event is written in the great book of the sky. This is how everything depends on the sky in the exchange of radiations and forms between sky and earth, but can also reverberate its own forces in the sky. If one only imitates the celestial figures in the appropriate talismans, and at the right time, then the influences come together and react, through the exceptional potential of the *miraculum magnum* which is man, and can, from mediation to mediation, capture and make use of every celestial power, by words and songs (the 'power of words and songs for obtaining heavenly benefit'). Ficino was to use all the astral 'images' in this way without impiety, the visible ones like the constellations, the invisible ones which can only be imagined, or the 'figures' (*facies*), 'divined, or at least devised, by the Indians, the Egyptians and the Chaldeans', and all those described by Albumasar and the others. The celestial powers are caught by the image (*simulacrum*) which imitates them when they are perfectly reproduced in suitable matter – but matter alone is not enough – and they exercise their effectiveness through the spirit. 'To fight a fever one sculpts Mercury in marble, in the hour of Mercury, when Mercury is rising, in the form of a man who bears arrows.' The practice of magic fits naturally into the universe, to make life more harmonious, by slowly correcting any alteration of rhythm according to the perfect order of the sky. 'It in fact would be as well to remember' – warns Ficino – 'that there is no excess of any of the properties of the elements in the sky . . . the most measured of all things, the sky rules all things, and reduces them to a unity.' 'Harmoniously formed, harmoniously moved, the sky does everything with a harmony of sound and movement, and through this sole harmony not only men, but all inferior things are prepared to receive the celestial gifts according to their capacity.'[22]

It is in this universal harmony that Ficino justifies astrology, together with magic, as being the concord of everything, in a concept which was to be so popular throughout the centuries, whilst the figures which peopled the heavens were transfigured into a fantastic vision of the cosmos, in the form of beauty which is also truth. Demons, gods, stars, prayers, all is music, beauty, harmony: all difficulties finally seem to be resolved under the sign of art. Music, the harmony of the world, the universal harmony, the eternal poem, the theatre of the world: these are all dominant themes from the fifteenth century onwards, and scientists and philosophers were to write and speak about them from Galileo to Kepler, from Descartes to Mersenne. 'De fabricanda universi figura' ('On making a figure of the universe') is the title of a chapter of the *Liber de vita* which is as controversial as it is emblematic. The world as a work of art could be the title of all Ficino's philosophy – the figured, animated, living world of the astrologers and the magicians. The world, indeed, which he wanted to reconstruct in its archetype when the Sun touches the first minute of Aries, or in that fatal hour which seals the fate of a world which is being reborn – when *sors quaedam quasi renascentis mundi revolvitur* (a certain destiny of the world as though being born again returns), as Ficino emphasises in an important passage. It is neither enough to build a perfect model of the world nor only to look at it: we must also bring it within ourselves through intense meditation ('not only contemplating but also refuting it in the mind') and the contemplation of its painted image in the rooms in which we live. Man the microcosm, that is, must adapt himself to the macrocosm through the technique of images, he must synthesise himself and so realise perfect harmony by identifying himself with the life and with the power of everything. Art and magic meet together ('we see compound things come alive when the perfect union seems to have done away with all preceding contradictions').[23]

It is indeed in discussing the picture of the world that

Ficino recalls Pico and the *Heptaplus*, that is the work in which Pico was both commenting on the biblical account of the creation and attempting a cabbalistic interpretation of it. I do not think one can separate the *Liber de vita*, with its construction of the image of the universe – the rebirth of the world (*sors mundi renascentis*) – from the atmosphere of the 1480s and 1490s, which was full of hermetic prophetism, of eschatological statements on the overthrow (*de eversione*) or the approach of Antichrist (*de adventu Antichristi*), no less than on renewal (*de renovatione*) and new eras, between conjunctions and fatal changes. These are the years of Mercurio da Correggio's hermetic prediction, and of Arquato's famous prophecy of the 'destruction of Europe'; these are the years in which Flavius Mithridates praised astrology, and when he presented Federigo, Duke of Urbino, with the translation from the Arabic of a text on celestial images (*Ali de imaginibus coelestibus*), he wrote, amongst other things: 'This is the divine science which makes men happy, which teaches them to appear gods among mortals: this science speaks with the stars, and, if one is allowed to say so, governs everything that is in the world with God.'[24]

There is certainly no need to quote further examples, however illustrious: but there was a movement of ideas, from magic to astrology, from Avicenna's interpretation of prophecies and miracles to the horoscope of religions, which seemed fundamentally to question the values of faith. The astrological versions of the star of the Magi, the Virgin as a celestial figure and the Cross as a talisman: all this swept away ancient beliefs, while the barriers between natural and supernatural were broken down. The result was basically the same whether everything was reduced to the natural or the supernatural, or whether all miracles were natural, or all nature was miraculous. It is indeed in this upheaval, and

in this atmosphere, that one finds Giovanni Pico della Mirandola's sensational yet tragic activity. He ended the century
with a very violent attack on divinatory astrology and false
prophets; he was the colleague and friend of Girolamo Savonarola, who was also an author of an anti-astrological text.
Ficino, Pico, Savonarola: for Ficino, Savonarola is the Anti-
christ prophesied by the stars; for Pico and his friends he is the
Ferrarese Socrates, a saintly and wise man who wants to
make Florence a new Jerusalem. For Savonarola astrology is
the destruction of Christianity, of the sense of Christ, of the
supernatural significance of faith; for Pico it is a mystifi-
cation of science and philosophy, a fatalistic vision of the
world, a religion masking as pseudo-rationality and disguised
as science.[25]

It is not easy to define the relationship between these three
men and their three positions. Was it Savonarola who stimulated Pico to fight the astrologers for defensive motives? Was
it Ficino who influenced the young Pico, and his early theses,
which were certainly openly aligned in defence of magic, and
which were not clear as regards astrology? It is not easy to say,
just as it is not easy to reconstruct a dialogue between Ficino
and Pico, which was more often filled with allusions than
with clear contrasts, and a path – that of Pico – whose first
stages lack sufficient documentation. The *Conclusiones* do
not allow one to see with certainty the personal position of
the young thinker, from which his evaluation of magic
emerges well, but that of astrology not as clearly. An important passage written by Andrew of Trebizond (George's
son) confirms that there was someone who not only distinguished them but also attacked them and precisely in Platonic circles. In the preface to his father's *Commentarium in
Almagestum*, a valuable copy of which was dedicated to
Sixtus IV, he attacks with extreme violence an unknown

Platonist, a 'novice' (*novicius*) who is accused of ignorance, of magic and – it seems – Jewish sympathies. Andrew of Trebizond's portrait could fit Pico, who even if he was not yet entirely Platonic in his thinking, nor bitterly anti-astro-logical, was certainly curious about Judaism; and was im-petuous, and he was often criticised for his youthful intemperance. One should perhaps suppose that Andrew was referring not to his works but to conversations, or to letters, which were well known, given the notoriety of the count who had already achieved a certain fame in 1484.[26]

On the other hand, many people have wanted to maintain that Pico was initially sympathetic to astrology, but they have not shown in their explanations that they know well enough how to distinguish between the different aspects and parts of the science of the stars. The traditional division between mathematical and divinatory, which is completely inadequate, only serves to generate confusion and ambi-guity. Neither did anyone seriously refute those celestial influences which were undeniable. The problem lay else-where and concerned general concepts of reality and history connected with astrological positions. If we find Pico closer in the *Heptaplus* itself to neoplatonism, and to Ficino, we also find a precise programme of criticism of astrology. 'Why are the stars in the firmament? . . . One should seek a dis-cussion with the astrologers who take confirmation of a science of divination from Moses having said that God put the stars there as signs', a statement condemned not only by Christians but also by Plato and Aristotle.

Pico, at the time of the *Heptaplus*, after the storm of con-demnation and his flight, is undoubtedly not the same Pico of his earlier writings, nor of his enthusiasm for the cabbalists; he is greatly changed and nothing prevents him from insisting that he has left behind his youthful attraction to the nexus of astrology–magic–cabbala. Only the decisive point is, if anything, another: which aspects of astrology, which interpretation of it, did Pico accept at the beginning? What was the route by which he came to revise his conceptions of magic and astrology? A careful reading of his texts, not ignoring the intense contemporary discussion, shows that he was always hostile to the theories of the conjunctions, far from 'naturalistic' interpretations of prophetic phenomena, convinced of the conflict between human liberty and astral determinism, persuaded of the difficulties in establishing causal relationships between general principles and individual events, loath to admit that that which is not the cause could be a sign.

It is possible that his ever-increasing closeness to Savonarola, and his prophetic experiences, had contributed to separating him not only from some of the beliefs of his youth but also from the 'mysteries' of Plato and Ficino. Furthermore, one must not forget his constant appreciation, from his early youth, of certain aspects of Aristotelianism, from logic to ethics, and his firm belief in human liberty, which was irreconcilable with the presuppositions of astrology. One notes however in his work, at the time of the *Disputationes* against the astrologers, a polemical tension which is so exasperated that one is reminded of Galileo's disbelief in action at a distance which brought him to deny the effect of the moon on the tides. Pico, after the long discussion about the subject, concluded firmly:

> Nothing forces us to admit that there is a new power in the Moon, other than movement and light, through which it moves the sea, since, having examined all the differences in the tides, it is evident that they have an obvious cause, either in the movement of the star which ascends or descends at the time, or in the growing and dimming of the light.

Here and elsewhere, in fact, his preoccupation is to accept only natural causes (*naturales causas*). That which cannot be reduced to natural causes (*redigere ad causas naturales*) is rejected. He did not in fact exclude the opportunity of adapting himself to the course of nature. He declared this on the subject of suitable times for medical cures and surgery ('works of art which are in harmony with the progression of nature are always more felicitous'). He denied every consideration of the heavens which was not in fact natural: he surreptitiously inserted a religion behind a scientific and geometric mask. Pico never denied that man as microcosm, being born from nature, is in harmony with the macrocosm; and he always recognised the sources of light, heat and movement in the stars. But this is not the point: and in the *Disputationes* it was put down with extreme clarity both on the plane of being and of knowledge. The stars are universal physical causes, inasmuch as they are considered regular and uniform in their movements, from which therefore particular effects cannot come down, without indeterminate mediations. Specific events cannot therefore be recognised through such general and remote causes. Many other arguments of different kinds were added to these about efficient causality, which constituted the theoretical skeleton of the *Disputationes*. And these were: the arguments against the occultists; the defence of human liberty against any assertion of destiny; the critical and historical analysis of astrological theories as a camouflage for astral cults and of general conceptions of the world which are linked to them; the defence of the Christian religion.

Pico observes in the prologue to the *Disputationes*, in a passage which is reminiscent of Giordano Bruno, and of his *Expulsion of the Triumphant Beast*, that divinatory astrology, having usurped the name and the appearance of the mathematical science of the heavens' movements, maintains that it can read human events in the mirror of the sky. 'But the mirror is too high for the images of earthly things to reach that far; its splendour is too brilliant for the weakness of our eye.' On the other hand the cloak of the astrologer's sky 'is embroidered with monstrous effigies instead of celestial ones, the stars are transformed into animals, and the whole sky is full of fables, and it is not the true heaven made by God but a false heaven, fashioned by the astrologers.' Bruno was to say that 'Jove . . . has filled the sky with so many beasts, as with so many vices, according to the form of the 48 famous images' – to be precise, the images of astrology. Pico also said: 'It is she . . . who corrupts philosophy, who poisons medicine, who weakens religion, who generates and re-enforces superstitions, who keeps idolatory alive, who destroys prudence, who sullies customs, who defames the sky, who makes men miserable, tormented and restive, who makes them servants and gives them an unhappy outcome to almost all their actions.'[27]

Chapter 4

The criticism of astrology and the natural history of the oracles

The importance of Pico should not be undervalued. The very angry reaction which constantly broke out against him is proof of the impact of his work. So Pomponazzi placed him side by side with Averroës in a very violent passage in the *De incantationibus*:

> The astrologers say things which are true in accordance with good sense and reason, whereas Averroës is seriously mistaken and contradicts good sense and reason . . . In the same way many modern writers make the same mistake as Averroës when they fight the astrologers with long and colourful arguments. Either they understand nothing about astrologers, or, if they do understand them, they are deeply mistaken. As for myself, I find only arrogance and impudence in their books, and there is nothing worthwhile in them apart from the elegant style. Many, indeed, maintain that these are not even their own arguments and that all they have done is to embellish them.

The same dubious accusation of plagiarism, or perhaps of a servile dependence on Savonarola, which is picked up by Pomponazzi in this statement, was widespread in Europe.[1] The truth, however, as far as Savonarola is concerned, is rather different. Savonarola compiled the *Trattato contra gli astrologi* late on, in 1497, and he declared it in the work itself,

where he emphasised that he had only just that moment read
Pico's book, in the posthumous edition: 'now that the book of
the *Disputationes* has been published . . . and having read
it . . .' Savonarola sums up Pico's work, at the same time
popularising, even though in a lively way, and adding something of his own to it, 'in corroboration of the astrological
refutations of Count Giovanni Pico della Mirandola', as he
adds in a phrase which was taken from the prologue and
appeared as a subtitle to the later editions of the *Trattato*.
One must add, however, that in the summer of 1494, in the
outlines of the predictions of Advent, Savonarola cites
Princeps contra astrologos ('The prince against the astrologers'), summing up an argument of the third chapter of the
third book of the *Disputationes*. It is in fact probable, as
Giovanni Nesi testifies in the *Oraculum de novo seculo*, that
between the end of 1493 and the beginning of 1494 Savonarola
helped his friend 'with advice and judgment' – as Ridolfi has
demonstrated – whilst he read or communicated to him his
own work as it came into being (*in fieri*).[2] Perhaps drawing
on Nesi, or perhaps from current rumours, the accusation of
dependence on Savonarola was renewed by Lucio Bellanti da
Siena, the bitter adversary of Pico and defender of astrology
in *De astrologica veritate et in disputationes Joannis Pici
adversus astrologos responsiones* which came out in Florence
in May 1498. There is nothing strange in the fact that Savonarola should have rested upon certain points of Pico's *Disputationes*. Savonarola was preoccupied with safeguarding
the autonomy of religion, the freedom of human will and the
supernatural nature of prophetic gifts. One thinks, after all,
of Luther's reaction to Melanchthon. However, Savonarola's
final thesis has a flavour typical of Pico:

> Speculative astrology is therefore a true science, because it
> tries to recognise the effects through the true causes . . . but

divinatory astrology which consists entirely of effects which proceed indifferently from their own causes, especially in human affairs which proceed from free will, and in those which rarely come from their causes, is wholly vain and can be called neither art nor science.

Here all Savonarola does is take up Pico's prologue:

When I say astrology I do not mean at all that which measures the size and clusters of the stars by mathematical methods, a sure and noble art, full of dignity through its own merits . . . but that which foresees the future from the path of the stars, deceitful speculation . . . supported by charlatans . . . whose followers were once called Chaldeans from their origins, or genethliacs from their profession.

That was a distinction which Pico always maintained; indeed, he had already observed in the *Conclusiones*, in an argument which sounds very similar to Galileo: 'Sicut vera Astrologia docet nos legere in libro Dei, ita Cabala docet nos legere in libro Legis.' ('Just as true Astrology teaches us to read in the book of God, so Cabbala teaches us to read in the book of Law.')

If this is the truth about the relationship between Savonarola's *Trattato* and Pico's *Disputationes*, the accusation of plagiarism hurled by Pomponazzi seems to have been no less widespread nor to have had a greater foundation. A. Gorfunkel found this annotation in a copy of the Strasbourg edition of Pico's works in 1504: 'Joannes Schonerus dicebat se vidisse antiquissimum librum apud episcopum Bambergensem manu scriptum ex quo Joannes iste Picus omnia descripsit, impudenter sibi ea vindicatus, quibus contra astrologos arbitratur. Liber autem ille ignoti auctoris erat.' ('Johann Schoener said that he had seen a very old manuscript in the library of the Bishop of Bamberg from which this

Giovanni Pico copied everything with which he testifies against the astrologers, shamelessly claiming it for himself. The author of this book, however, is unknown.') The diffusion of the knowledge of this annotation was attributed to 'George Joachim Rheticus the famous mathematician and doctor', who said that he had heard it in person. It is likely that Pico's supposed source, slanderously indicated as a plagiarised model, could be identified in one of the medieval writings against the astrologers which have been mentioned, from Oresme to Henry of Assia, which Pico himself praised.[3]

However, we wished to underline the bitterness of the polemic which tried to attack Pico from two sides: on that of magic, through his defence, especially in his youth, of natural magic against ritual magic; on that of astrology once again, through his defence of astronomy against the art of the horoscopes. In other words, it is precisely Pico's effort to distinguish the rational element from the mythical element which is the centre of the debate. Pico tries, in many areas of learning, to isolate truly scientific aspects and methods from intrusions of any other kind; superstitions, mystical intuitions, relics of all kinds of beliefs. And this is the particularly notable importance of his work which, not by chance, was prepared for publication by a famous sixteenth-century doctor, Giovanni Mainardi. It was destined to stimulate discussions for more than a century which concerned, as well as astronomy and the physical sciences, medicine and human knowledge in general. It was not only a question of research into the causes of extraordinary effects on the one hand, and the bases of horoscopes and prognostications, both general and particular, on the other. It was a matter of investigating the causal links, the nature of celestial influences, the crises both of historical processes and the life of individuals (the parallel, which we read in Machiavelli, between the phen-

omena of individual life and the life of peoples is common).
One finds then, along with the philosophy of history, politics
and morality, medicine and biology, and the fundamental
concepts of natural sciences, from that of causality to that of
law, entering into the discussion about astrology again. And
obviously religion is involved and whatever concerns mental
life. It is not by chance that Giovanni Pico's nephew, Gianfrancesco della Mirandola, a prominent figure in the first
decades of the sixteenth century, links his analysis of astrology, which had been taken from Giovanni Pico, to a critical
analysis of the bases of knowledge in general, and of the
various arts and disciplines. His *Examen vanitatis doctrinae
gentium*, whose distant echoes are still recognisable in the
great philosophy of the seventeenth century, tackles a true
and proper questioning of the tools of knowledge and science
by means of a revival of Sextus Empiricus and a re-evaluation
of sceptical arguments. Sense and reason, space and time,
cause and movement, finite and infinite: the significance and
validity of all the central notions of human knowledge are in
some way investigated through the alteration of classical
philosophies.[4]

If we run through Giovanni Pico's *Disputationes*, with
which the fifteenth century seems to close, we realise the
reasons for their influence, and for the programmatic statement of their author: that they dealt with freeing not just one
particular aspect of human life from ambiguity, but every
field of knowledge and action. The initial arguments of the
work, which on first reading seem to be simply rhetorical,
prove instead to be very precise: it is not only about the
restoration of the liberty and dignity of the will, about re-
instating trust and responsibility in action, about purifying
religious life: it is concerned with giving new life to medicine,
converting it from superstition to a science; in general it is a

matter of reforming philosophy. In other words, and Pico says this with extreme clarity in the final part of his book, divinatory astrology is not to be fought as scientific error, or not only to be fought in this way: it has to be identified in its real nature as a general conception of reality, and as a religious vision, which, as such, introduces the concepts which derive from it into every aspect of human life. He asks:

> If astrological fables are not founded on reason, and its experiments are not to be trusted, why should the wise man acknowledge them? Or perhaps we have to believe them to be oracles? And shall we accept as divine the things which we have disproved as irrational, imitating the astrologers who refer all the things men do to the stars without reason? Shall we follow their example and refer men's deliria to the gods?

It is particularly worth noting Pico's effort, throughout the twelfth book of the *Disputationes*, to reconstruct the history of astrology as the progressive influx of religious beliefs of ancient peoples, such as the Egyptians and the Chaldeans, into the realm of philosophy and science – a confusion which seemed to him to have happened by no accident in the field of astronomy, due to the constant ambiguity between real physical bodies and stellar divinities. Pico observed:

> Though the Greek philosophers thought correctly on the subject of natural philosophy through rational demonstrations, in no way have they drawn from the Egyptians; they have only taken things regarding cults and astronomy from the Egyptians. And the proof of this is that they always cite the Chaldeans and Egyptians when talking about astronomy and the mysteries . . . but in philosophical discussions we never see them mentioned beside Plato or Aristotle.

On the other hand, Pico continues, it is not difficult to realise the mental process through which astrology became a

general, unitary conception of reality among the Egyptians
and Chaldeans. He wrote in an eloquent passage:[5]

> How many people are immersed in a theory, are used to
> reducing everything to it, and not because of a desire to
> explain everything by it, but because things really seem
> like that to them. What happens to them is like someone
> who walks immersed in snow and to whom everything ends
> up appearing white . . . like someone who loves in vain and
> sees the face of his beloved in everything . . . So he who is a
> theologian, and nothing but a theologian, takes everything
> back to divine causes; he who is a doctor takes every-
> thing back to corporal states, the physician to the natural
> principles of things, the mathematician to numbers and
> figures, like the Pythagoreans. In the same way, as the
> Chaldeans were entirely occupied with the measurement
> of celestial movements and the observation of the positions
> of the stars . . . all things were stars to them, and they
> willingly took everything back to the stars.

Astrology had thus become a general conception of reality,
and, as such, the roots of the tree of knowledge. So Pico
follows it consistently in every field beginning with very
general questions about logic and metaphysics. The astrologers[6]

> have not considered physical reality sufficiently, so as to
> completely to understand what distinguishes the universal
> cause from the particular one, what is the function of this
> and of that, what brings together and what repulses the
> substance of the heavens, what is substance and what is
> contingency . . what difference there is between the works
> of nature and those of human art, if a sign can indicate a
> thing without being its cause.

The theoretical framework which Pico opposed to the
astrological vision of reality would merit a close examination, as that which could form a chapter of that agreement,

or harmony, between Platonism and Aristotelianism, which the philosopher pursued from the time of his early studies. Aristotelian is the insistence on the impossibility of deriving particular cases from universal causes, but the defence of the infinite possibilities of the human mind has a neo-platonic flavour. On the other hand his continual polemic against the Egyptians and Chaldeans, and above all against Egyptian cults, is perhaps a hidden attack on Ficino – at least against a certain Egyptian fashion which Ficino's hermeticism had launched.

Central themes of Pico's refutation were the connection between medicine and astrology, with regard to childbirth at eight months, critical days and lunar influences; the theory of the tides; the doctrine of 'elections'; the great conjunctions with the horoscope of Christ and of religions in general; the question of the nature of the celestial forces, light, heat and motion. At the centre is the re-emergence of the theme of autonomy, or rather of the sovereignty of man, as soul, mind and constructive free will, with respect to material nature. The greatness of Aristotle is not explained by celestial causes: and not only because many men were born under the same signs who were not Aristotle, but because Aristotle's mind is outside the chain of natural causes. Pico says to the astrologer:

> You admire in Aristotle a perfect science and I admire it with you. Its cause, you say, is in the heavens and the stellar configurations under which Aristotle was born. I deny this: and not so much for the banal reason that many who were born under the same star are not Aristotle, as because besides the heavens, under which both the swine of Boeotia and the Attic philosophers are born as if from a universal cause, there are closer causes of his own, peculiar to Aristotle, to which we can refer Aristotle's singular merit . . . It was his fate to have a good soul and it was not

given to him by the heavens . . . and a body . . . and this too was not from the heavens, but from his parents . . . The intelligence, which is not corporeal, does not come from a star, but from God, just as his body came to him from his father and not from the heavens.

Pico, as an enemy of general causes without middle terms, assigns precisely the search for mediations and near causes to science. As an enemy of occult causes and demons, Pico points to human liberty as a constructive capacity, through natural magic. Certainly when he was drawing up his *Disputationes* between 1493 and 1494, his interest had shifted in relation to when he responded to the accusations of the Roman theologians defending magic with the Cabbala. He wrote in the *Apologia*:

I say and I repeat that this name 'magic' is an ambiguous term, and means either necromancy, in which one acts through strict pacts and agreements with demons, or the practical part of the science of nature, which only teaches us to achieve admirable works by means of natural forces, connecting one with the other, and making them act on passive natures.

His attitude had him condemned, besides the voluminous refutation of Pedro Garcia in 1489 (*Determinationes magistrales contra conclusiones apologiales*). Here the future Bishop of Barcelona touched on an important point, among other things, perhaps indeed the most serious aspect of the question: namely the relationship between the theoretic moment of knowledge of universal causes (astronomy) and the practical, experimental moment (magic). The *noticia experimentativa quae circa singularia et singulares circumstantias versatur* ('experimental knowledge which is concerned with particular things and circumstances') can never be a science and can only be treacherous and erroneous (*in pluribus deceptiones et errores*). To consider the *noticia experimentativa* (experimental knowledge) as being *scientia* (a science), or *pars scientiae naturalis* (part of natural science), is *ridiculum* (ridiculous). The magician is called *experimentator* (an experimenter) not a *sciens* (a scientist). In other words the mediation which Pico was looking for between astrology (and the Cabbala) and magic, or between the theoretical moment and the practical moment, is illusory. There is not, and there cannot be, a dialectical relationship. Obviously Pico believed that he had given an answer in the *Oratio* with the *miraculum magnum*, with man who makes and makes himself, who is the mediator of the worlds, knowledge and action. This does not dispense with the difficulties from the point when, in the *Disputationes* themselves, he reaffirmed the Aristotelian image of the heavens as universal causes, which could be recognised by reason, in antithesis to the world of the particular, experimental, individual and variable, which is neither determined *a priori*, nor, therefore, an area for any scientific operation. The major limitation of Pico's *Disputationes* is not at all, as is still repeated, Ptolemaic geocentrism, which is for the most part very vague: it is the Aristotelian antithesis between heaven and earth, between the physics of the heavens and the physics of the earth. It is both the illusion of overcoming the connection between the world of necessity and the world of freedom with the appeal to the *miraculum magnum*, after having stressed the distance between matter and soul, between fate and free will.[7]

With all this, in fact precisely because of all this, the *Disputationes* remain a great cultural event: for the stimulus they gave on the theoretical plane, to the foundation of science, by questioning the central points of our knowledge of the universe ('*de caelo et mundi*' ('about the heavens and the earth')); for its reminder of the urgency of realising that astrology, which permeated customs and the whole of life with its concepts, was, not so much a technique of prediction as a general conception of reality and of history, and was always present and decisive. The belief in stellar fate worked everywhere, from the daily customs to medical practice, from artistic representations to solemn prayers, from the concept of cycles in history to religious themes. Pico's massive book, though neither finished nor polished, came out posthumously amidst apocalyptic announcements and imminent catastrophies, and was a great recall to reason and to the liberty of man and an act of faith in the possibility of criticism and of historical research. By forcing a debate on astrology, he invited a close discussion on astronomy, or rather on the physical universe and on man, on nature and on destiny. This discussion is placed alongside the debate on the soul and on immortality, initiated by Ficino and Pomponazzi, and that on human society and on the state which was dramatically expressed by Machiavelli. They are three explosive themes: and it is not perhaps accidental that the three problems were to come out almost at the same time and in the same places, and that this was not without all kinds of reciprocal interconnections and links. They are, on the other hand, the focal points of the philosophical 'revolution' of the modern age: the order of the world: the concept of the self: the *res publica*, the state.[8]

It would be interesting to follow in detail, in all its particular developments, the fortune of Pico's work, at least throughout the sixteenth century: but it would be a never-ending task. One need only think of a single point: that is, the problem which was so important for doctors, of crises and of critical days, which had immediate repercussions, not only on cures and medications, but on surgical operations – and on their timing in general. Girolamo Fracastoro, to mention but one, brought to light very clearly the need to determine if the crises, the critical days and the rhythms of life in general, could be taken back to celestial causes – for example the Moon – or instead to internal causes (as he was inclined to believe), or to a periodicity inherent in the phenomena of life. That is to say nothing about the arguments on epidemics and contagion.[9] Pico was certainly not the first to raise such questions but he had linked them together and at the same time he had indicated how a serious solution would require a general theoretical re-examination, which involved on the one hand logic as well as metaphysics, and which, on the other hand, in its consequences, concerned the great themes of religion and politics. Religion was not seriously under-mined only by those who presented it as a political instru-ment, but also by those who subordinated it to the move-ments of the heavens, reducing it to the dimensions of an eclipse (and often the two attitudes converged).

Obviously it was easy to attack him by emphasising only certain apologetic themes in his works and making capital of his link with Savonarola. Or else, rather than disprove him, show the poetical aspect of astrology in all its seductive fascination, as Pontano, among others, did so eloquently, and insist on the heavens as being signs (*segni*) more than causes (*cause*): 'the heavens tell of the glory of God.'[10] It was this, an insistence on the aspect of 'the return to the ancients', which was the least innovatory, which redis-covered the much purer and more fascinating features of the Greek gods beneath their fearful and barbaric deformities. When Cornelius Agrippa came to divinatory astrology in his well known *Declamatio de incertitudine et vanitate scien-tiarum atque artium*, after observing that Bellanti's discus-sions had not even scratched the surface of Pico's arguments, he then declared that all divination boiled down on the one hand to poetry and on the other to lucrative charlatanism. But he was also to add, almost paraphrasing Pico, that astrology, or better still the astrological concept of reality, not only subverted religion by denying providence, but corrupted all the good arts (*bonae artes*), above all philosophy and medicine, but also the ethical disciplines by substituting 'fables' for 'real causes', and so corrupting morality. It is not easy, obviously, to judge Agrippa's position exactly, from the famous magical organisation in the *De occulta philosophia* to the 'declamation' on uncertainty (*de incertitudine*), even if it suggests a kind of dialectical relationship between the two themes. One thing, however, is fairly clear: that Pico's *Disputationes* forced many to rethink and to examine the validity of the sciences. And if the harmonious and musical visions continued of a whole which is ordered in grades and on corresponding levels along the lines of Ficino and hermeticism (one need only think of Francesco Zorzi), if magic was to follow its dreams of action and of mastering reality, Pico's theories gave rise to increasingly worrying questions. Among which, as has already been mentioned, is that of Gian Francesco Pico who, starting from the problem of 'foresight', and the arts which pretend to know the future in general, intended to complete Giovanni Pico's plan, confronting the problem of the foundations and logical and methodological processes of the 'disciplines'. He did not want to come out like Agrippa with a declamation of uncertainty (*declamatio de incertitudine*), but he wanted instead to focus on the bases of knowledge by analysing its possibilities.[11]

There had certainly been no lack of 'comparisons' (*paragoni*) between the 'arts' before Gian Francesco, nor of classifications and trees of the sciences and the arts, discussions on their nobility, even if located in the object or on the level of certainty. There had also been attempts at 'logical' discussions. Pico, however, was impelled by two pressing questions: one religious – whether philosophy leaves room, and how much, for faith; the other completely theoretical – if human sciences are possible, and what they are based on. It is equally important that it was the ancient sceptics, and Sextus Empiricus himself, who stimulated him. Gian Francesco Pico in fact fully developed the teaching of the *Disputationes*: he went beyond disproving a pseudo-science, and the examination of its historical foundation, to confront in depth the problem of the possibilities and of the limits of human knowledge, taking up again the analysis of the great philosophical-scientific inheritance of the past: the 'learning of the nations' (*doctrina gentium*). Even here one ends up with an 'emptiness' (*vanitas*), as Agrippa did afterwards: but Agrippa was to end his youthful exaltation of magic and the occult with a 'declamation full of invective' (*invectiva declamatio*), whereas Pico with a quite different consistency related the destruction of a false science to a critique of its foundations.

Pietro Pomponazzi, in direct opposition to Pico, and also with Gian Francesco, confronted the problems of astrology, of magic, and in the same way of religions, miracles and oracles in general, in a work which was to be influential because of its subversive nature. The *De incantationibus*, or better, the *De naturalium effectuum causis sive de incantationibus*, is a work which one cannot understand – as it has often not been understood – unless one connects it with the problems of causality, of heavenly causes, of occult causes, of exceptional and marvellous events, of religions and of their variations. Pomponazzi did not conceal who the work was intended for. Ficino and Pico are explicitly declared; others are not difficult to recognise: doctors like Antonio Benivieni, who was preoccupied with discussing 'some hidden and marvellous causes of diseases and cures' (*de abditis nonnullis ac mirandis morborum et sanationum causis*) or like Andrea Cattani, who was intent on dealing *de causis mirabilium effectuum* ('with the causes of miraculous effects').[12] In the background are the efforts of Avicenna and his followers to give a natural explanation not only for dreams and prophecies, but for *incantatio* (enchantment), and *fascinatio* (bewitching), and every marvellous and miraculous effect by means of the imagination. An explanation was sought for all experience, normal or otherwise, including miracles and prophecies and prognostications, through natural causes if it were possible. So on the one hand, astrology and magic, and on the other, religions were examined.

It is important to realise straight away Pomponazzi's position on this subject, especially with regard to Pico. He had wanted to explain Pico's natural causes rationally, but he broke up the unity of reality by emphasising the ontologically exceptional nature of man when faced with the risk of seeing man absorbed back into nature and so subject to fate. I do not think it is possible to understand Pico's theory without concentrating on his interpretation of the *magnum miraculum* (great miracle), of the *copula mundi* (bond of the world), of man as the intermediary and link of reality. The liberty of man is in fact justified by destroying the unity of the whole. Man does not come back into the ontological structure of reality. In this sense Pico moved away from Ficino as well as Pomponazzi. Ficino exalts in man a reality which is already raised in a unitary way to life and soul as a result of his exasperation at giving life and soul to the whole of reality. In Pomponazzi's work which, on the contrary, reduces man to nature, and thus links him to necessity and binds him to an animal nature, one recognises nevertheless that man has a kind of exceptional morality. From this comes the tragedy of

the wise who are conscious of the vanity of life like Prom-
etheus tied to the rock and devoured by the vulture. It is the
nobility of man who knows he is going to die and dreams of
immortality. The compact structure of reality is only broken
'morally'. So, somehow, it is the same as Ficino's unitary
universe which tends to reincorporate and in the end make
vain everything in the soul (and the body is only a shadow of
this): it is symmetrical, even if reversed to Pomponazzi's
universe in which everything is mortal corporality ('and the
immortality of the soul is only a fragrance and a dream).[13]

Pomponazzi himself observed in a passage in *De fato, de
libero arbitrio et de praedestinatione*, which was finished
almost at the same time as *De incantationibus* in 1520, that
the whole world rises and falls in successive cycles, speaking
about the inevitable change of the world and of fortune, or of
the infinite 'vicissitudes' of which Giordano Bruno also spoke
so often:

> He who before, at one time, was a beggar, at another time
> will be a king or a master . . . Cities and countries which
> were large and powerful later become small and weak . . .
> Thus it all seems to be a game of the gods (*ludus deorum*).
> For this reason Plato said that as man is a miracle of nature
> (*miraculum in natura*), he did not know whether God
> made him seriously or as a joke (*ludo an serio*).

The *miraculum magnum* certainly, but without breaking the
structure of being, the laws of nature, which would be contradictory, absurd and impossible: so, yes, man is a 'miracle
of nature', but one of pure illusion and suffering: *ludis
deorum*, a game of the gods.[14]

Pomponazzi too, like Pico and Ficino, whom he kept in
mind, tackles the problem of magic and astrology, but in
order to insert both of them into a rigidly naturalistic and
fatalistic concept of things. His use, for the most part highly

critical, of Avicenna's work too is turned to utilising
certain of its suggestions with a view to an explanation in
terms of natural causes for the so-called wonderful effects of
nature, and of the influence the imagination or the emotions
can have on the physical plane, in such a way as to determine
organic changes which are taken to be exceptional or miraculous.

In this general concept of things, the picture, so to speak, of
the whole is the natural order, the order of things (*ordo
rerum*), the 'successive and perpetual vicissitudes' of things,
the transformation of things and beings, one into the other,
their death and rebirth in unending cycles, always different
and always the same. In concluding *De fato*, Pomponazzi
said:[15]

> That order will exist always in infinite ages, to infinity: it
> is not in our power, but in the power of fate . . . And as we
> see that the earth which is now fertile will be barren, and
> the great and the rich will become humble and wretched,
> so the course of history is determined. We have seen the
> Greeks dominate the Barbarians, now the Barbarians dom-
> inate the Greeks, and so everything goes on and changes. So
> it is probable that he who is now a king will one day be a
> slave, and vice versa . . . If then someone asks you, what
> kind of game is this? You would be well advised to reply
> that it is the game of God (*Quis ludus est iste? . . . Dei ludus
> esse*).

Having established this eternal and universal vicissitude of
things, this perennial cycle of ascent and descent, the revival
of astrology with all its great themes follows logically from
it: from the movement of civilisation to the changing of
religions: '*Corpora coelestia . . . universum gubernant et
conservant.*' ('The heavenly bodies . . . govern the universe
and conserve it.') Pomponazzi appeals to a kind of common

consensus, from the theses of Jacques Lefèvre d'Étaples to that of the Etruscan soothsayers.[16]

> The Etruscan soothsayers stated . . . in fact that there are eight different kinds of life and customs. God has assigned everyone a period of time in the cycle of the great year. When a period comes to its end, and the next one is already imminent, signs are produced in both the earth and the heavens which can show the appearance of men who are destined to live with different customs and rules, with greater or lesser favour from the gods to those investigators who are expert in such things. Moreover, great revolutions (*magnas immutationes*) take place with every change in life.

Apart from specific cases, Pomponazzi has no doubts concerning the celestial connection, and therefore the determination on the part of the stars, of all human events. If the *ordo rerum*, the perennial 'vicissitude', involves the universe in natural cycles, why should not a revolution or the birth of a great man be inserted like emergent links in the long chain of events?[17]

> Furthermore I cannot ever remember having read in history books that any notable political change, or the life of any man worth mentioning, be it because of his virtue or his wickedness, did not take place without having those great celestial portents present at birth or at death, at the beginning or the end. And since such portents are given always or frequently, then they must have a natural cause. Furthermore it can also be argued that they draw from the power of celestial bodies from the fact that, as the histories tell, the astrologers forecast them or interpret them on the basis of the observation of the stars.

Once the prejudicial metaphysics of a human world which is apart have been destroyed, in a freedom which has been released from destiny, not only is the celestial clock presented as a great calculating machine which regulates the whole future of the universe, but earthly experiences are also called upon to prove the connection which operates between heaven and earth. If everything is linked together, both a great saint and a great wrongdoer are the earthly transcriptions of heavenly events. What matters to Pomponazzi is to bring every apparently abnormal phenomenon back into the sphere of rational interpretation and natural causes. Not demons nor miracles, but nervous tension, force of the imagination, powers and qualities which are occult not because they are supernatural but because they have not yet been understood: these are the causes of miraculous events:[18]

And here is an exemplary testimony. Many people in Padua came together in the court of the bishop, Pietro Barozzi, who was not only a very gifted but also a very saintly man. Whilst in the bishop's presence, the conversation turned to Apollonius of Tyana who was able to see very distant things. Many attributed this power to the art of magic. That very cultured man, who was universally esteemed among the most expert in the mathematical disciplines, smiled and said that he did not see anything in all this which was not according to nature. In fact, things in the lower world give out images and forms into the air, right up to the heavens, and from there they are reflected and reverberated down to the lower zones, as from one mirror to another. In such a way objects can be seen in the distance. He also cited authors who had affirmed this, but I cannot remember them; he added many stories on the subject and said that some of them had been believed to be saints for such things, but they would rather have been worthy of being considered devils for the faults they committed.

Pomponazzi does not deny natural magic, in as much as he does not deny the effects of unknown human qualities and powers. Just as certain herbs, or certain smells, produce medicinal or physiological effects, why cannot certain men act in a similar way? Why not admit that the tension of the imagination, or of the emotions, influences the body producing changes such as the stigmata, or such like? ('Doctors and philosophers know how far faith and imagination are effective.') So according to Pomponazzi when the citizens of L'Aquila were united in fervent prayer to San Celestino, which sent away the storm, they succeeded in effecting a physical process similar to that which one obtains by ringing the tocsin bells: that is movements and changes in the air, which moved the clouds. And he comments:

> One calls it magic because only the most knowledgeable among men understand it, and the most secret things belong to the knowledgeable (*occultissima sunt sapientum*) . . . and the term 'magician' in Persian means 'sage' . . . It is for the people that angels and demons have been introduced, and those who introduced them know very well that they could never exist . . . But common men who are not philosophers are in reality like beasts (*veluti bestiae*) . . . As Averroës says in his *Poetics*, the language of religions (*sermo legum*) is similar to that of the poets . . . Such fables serve to lead us to truth and to instruct the ignorant rabble that it is right to aim at good and shun evil, just as one does with children by the hope of reward and the fear of punishment.

Religions are useful on the pedagogic, social and political plane and because of their rites and prayers they are also effective.

> One is wrong, therefore, to accuse philosophers of impiety, and to say that according to them it would be futile to pray to the gods . . . On the contrary, it is obvious that according to the philosophers one must pray to the gods, that prayer is never futile.

102

It is important, however, to realise when one religion is dying and when another is being born. When a religion is waning the effects of prayers are weakened (*frigescunt*), and miracles do not happen any more.[19] In a passage which was famous for the scandal which it roused through the centuries, Pomponazzi translated his theory on the changes of religions into an almost brutal form, which was later the astrological theory of the horoscope of religions:[20]

> As the change in religion is the greatest of all changes, and as the step from something which is usual to something which is absolutely unusual is difficult, the succession of a new religion must be accompanied by extraordinary and bewildering miracles. For this reason the heavenly bodies make men appear who can perform miracles at the approach of a new religion. So such men can make rains, hailstorms and earthquakes appear or disappear, they can command the winds and the sea, they can cure every kind of illness, they can unveil secrets, predict the future and remember the past, go beyond the common sensibility of men. Otherwise they could not introduce such diverse new religions and customs. So the forces which are spread through the herbs, stones and rational and irrational animals, seem to be focused in them through the gift of God and the intelligences, so much so that they are rightly thought to be the sons of God (*Dei filii rationabiliter creduntur*).

For the same reasons, at the time when Christianity was being born the sign of the cross cured illnesses but does not do so any more today. 'For this reason everything today is cold in our religion, and there are no more miracles, unless they are false and deceptive: for the end seems near.' The end of a cycle, obviously – the end of Christianity, not the absolute end:

> After all these oracles will arise others of a kind opposite to

the preceding ones; but the first category will not perish absolutely . . . as when the menstrual blood is corrupted, and a man is born from it, nature is not deprived of menstrual blood for ever, it is just that that blood has taken human form.

Certainly Pomponazzi made use of Plutarch, but the crudeness with which he puts together the horoscope of religions, and the theory of the religions as being fictions to govern peoples, makes an impression. Vanini faithfully transcribed this blasphemous passage in the 52nd dialogue, *de oraculis* of the *De admirandis naturae arcanis*. The gods die because they are born, even if they will be reborn in the eternal cycle ('cum . . . *Dii . . . habeant deficere quoniam incoeperunt, veluti corrumpitur sanguis menstrualis*' ('For . . . the gods . . . have to cease since they began, just as menstrual blood is corrupted'); their image 'broken and useless' remains in the meantime 'cold and dead'.[21] Robert Burton was to comment in the *Anatomy of Melancholy*:[22]

> Caesar Vaninus . . . is more free, copious and open . . . than any of our modern writers, Cardan excepted. A true disciple of his master Pomponatius; according to the doctrine of perapatetics, he refers all apparitions, prodigies, miracles, oracles, accidents, alterations of religions, kingdoms, etcetera (for which he is soundly lashed by Marinus Mercennus, as well he deserves), to natural causes.

However in the eighteenth century the controversy was to shift, even though the inheritance of those full pages of Pomponazzi, passed on by the atheist Vanini, was to play an active part in all the discussions about the libertines.[23]

We have not discussed Cardano, and many others with him, Nifo for example – both in Italy and abroad.[24] In fact the most burning questions of the astrological debate all found a model expression in the dialogue between Ficino, Pico and

Pomponazzi: it is not by chance that it is those passages which most frequently turn up in the discussions of the following centuries. Somehow a historical period ended with that dialogue. These original and important theories were to be put down in different terms later on: on a scientific basis, on the basis of astronomy as a science; on the basis of the philosophy of history and human society.

Pomponazzi says at a certain point, and not without a certain note of disparagement, that religion, inasmuch as it is the medicine of the soul, makes use of poetic language.

> For this reason I am inclined to think, and I believe that I am not far from the truth here, that Plato introduced angels and demons, not because he believed in their existence but because his purpose was to instruct common men. In fact, as Aesculapius was a doctor of bodies so Plato was a doctor of human souls.

And a little further on:

> The Platonic method of philosophising by means of enigmas, metaphors and images, which Plato used very frequently, was condemned by Aristotle who completely rejected it. No wonder that Plato was exalted by the ignorant and by priests, while Aristotle on the other hand was rejected and discredited.

Pomponazzi was probably referring here specifically to Ficino who spoke of himself in the *De vita* as a 'priest' (*sacerdos*), a pupil of Plato 'the doctor of souls' (*medicus animorum*). However, a strange poetic text of the sixteenth century leads us back to Plato and Ficino as well as to Lucretius on the subject of astrology. This text was published in the period 1534–7 and was called the *Zodiacus vitae*. It was a Latin poem written in hexameters whose rather mysterious author, Marcellus Palingenius Stellatus, or Pier Angelo

105

Manzolli of La Stellata near Ferrara, was actually identified with Ficino in the eighteenth century. This identification is obviously far-fetched and is perhaps due to the puns in the *De vita* where Ficino says he has been reborn (*renatus*), thus becoming 'Palingenius'; however the resemblance of certain themes (Lucretius and the Platonists), and certain general opinions are not so strange. Astrology is indeed poetry above all in the *Zodiacus vitae*, and the sky is populated with spirits and divinities and becomes an archetypal zone of superior beauty. 'A . . . poem . . . which is typically "Renaissance", full . . . of "platonic" metaphysics and pagan mythology . . . profoundly influenced by the revival of "platonism" and neo-platonism of the fifteenth century, after the fashion of Ficino': this is what Alexander Koyré wrote, who acknowledged 'the honour of having asserted the infinity of the universe',[25] in Palingenius. The stars therefore order the rhythm of life: ('What vertue hath the skye? / All force and vertue in the starres and glittering planets lye. / The Starres do guide the caupast world, and every change doth bring / The Starres create all things on earth and govern every thing' (tr. B. Googe, op.cit. in n.30, p.213).[26] Different from each other, different in their positions, the stars define the various configurations in the sky: 'Sereno / quae passim coelo veneranda luce refulgent. Ex quibus astronomi varias fecere figuras, / et finxere amplum diversis aethera signis.'[27] 'That in the cleare nights amyd the skyes with gorgeous light do shine: / Of which th'Astronomers have framde, faire shapes and figures bright, / And pictured have the Heavens brave with signes of sundrie sight' (ibid., p.214). The whole of the heavens is the face of Nature: powerful Nature which governs the entire universe. Palingenius says:[28]

I Nature call the fixed law of him that guides the skie, /

Which from the worldes foundation first to all things be assured, / And willde that it should stand in force, while age of world endured, / For this same law hath God unto, the formes of things assignde, / That when from thence do things procede, formes will fulfil Gods minde, / Or can they once this order breake. For of their formes do spring / Such things as he commaunded hath, who framde each formed thing. (Ibid., p.217)

The heavens truly constitute the 'face of the whole universe' (*facies totius universi*) of Spinoza; the archetypal source of everything is placed in the heavens. ('There must be placed the seeds and causes of all things. The sensible world must gush out, as from a spring, from that spiritual archetype of which it is only an imperfect image.') The tendency to humble the earth and the sublunar world even more as a zone of shadow and evil compared to the levels of celestial perfection, is striking in Palingenius's work. Life itself, blessed and perfect life, is there, in the infinite space of the ether, in the divine cities.[29]

For creatures doth the skies containe, and every starre beside / Be heavenly towns and seates of saints, where King, and Commons bide, / But perfect kings and people eke, all things are perfect there: / Not shapes and shadowes vaine of things (as we have present here), / Which death soon takes, and time destroyes, defiles, and drives away. / There, wise and happy folkes, and such as never do decay / Do live, here misers dwell and men that certaine are to die, / And doltish fooles. There peace and light, and pleasure chiefe doth lye: / Here daily warres, and darknesse blinde, and every kind of paine. (Ibid., p.218)

Aude, o demens, stabulum hoc praeponere coelo – exclaims Palingenius – *totius mundi stabulum Terra* [Presume, thou foole, than Heavens faire, the earth to set more by. Earth is stable to all the worlde.'] (Googe, p.218)

Rosemond Tuve has even spoken of an almost Manichean dualism in Palingenius's work. One is probably dealing with a strong Lucretian influence, which transforms – not misconstrues, as Yates would have it – the contrast between the serene *intermundia* (spaces between the worlds) and worldly trouble.[30] A transformation in which the neoplatonic influence plays a decisive role. However, the sense of destiny as a rule governing the theatre of the world remains ('nature rejoices in such differences which decorate the Theatre of the World in diverse ways'), and of this ideal heaven, of these adamantine worlds which are traversed by intelligent creatures, of this fantasy which peoples the cities of the heavens in ways which are worthy of the land of Ariosto.[31] A grand fable remains which has celestial images as its characters and is full of moral rather than metaphysical meanings. It is above all a great poetic fresco which vanishes in a dream. The professional astrologers continue to compose horoscopes, but Astolfos and Hippogriffs fly in the heavens of the *Zodiacus vitae*.

In its last flowering in the Renaissance, to tell the truth, astrology came to inspire once more not only fantastic transfigurations and pictorial images: it fostered the construction of 'theatres' of memory such as those of Giulio Camillo Delminio, that is techniques of the art of memory; and even projects of moral and religious reform, such as those of Giordano Bruno: between the 'shadows of the ideas' and the 'expulsions of the triumphant beast'.

In recent times scholars have come to Giulio Camillo, who not by chance was sung of by Ariosto too, turning their attention to several aspects: as Cabbalist (as such he was studied by François Secret), as theorist of rhetoric and imitation (Bernard Weinberg and Paola Barocchi have examined and published him under this aspect). Frances Yates, on the other hand, has given particular attention to his art of memory. But it is indeed another ambition which characterises the construction of his *Theatro*; he wanted to base mnemonics not only on imaginative links but on the exact symmetry of the various planes of the ontological structure of reality. Places and images draw their effectiveness from occult correspondences, grasped in their authenticity. Thus Camillo refers in the *Discorso* to Trifon Gabriele, to Avicenna's thesis on the power of the soul 'to change things' if it is only 'moved by some great emotion'. The links between the levels of reality – between signs and the thing signified – in Camillo's work are occult powers and active forces; the astrological images like the symbols of the talismans have practical repercussions and evocative powers. An astrological 'sign', precisely because it condenses fundamental energies, activates a whole series of relationships, be it on the mental or on the physical level. For this reason the *Theatro* is not only a treatise on topics or mnemotechnics, it is also a magical, astrological and metaphysical compilation. Camillo writes that 'the great emotion', or mental tension, 'changes the body, and those things over which the body moves . . . through the dignity of Man . . . whom all inferior things obey.' It is important to define the system of signs and its code. For Camillo it is a question above all of celestial signs.

> When these signs have been gathered together according to an organic order and impressed on the memory by their images and symbols, the mind can move away from this middle celestial world in both directions: above, towards the super-celestial world of the Ideas, of the sephirot, of the angels, even entering Solomon's Temple of Knowledge; below, towards the sub-celestial or elementary world

which is ordered in the steps of the Theatre . . . in harmony with astral influences.

If, finally, the soul manages to harmonise with the great celestial machine through the images and forces which fill it, it will also manage to penetrate all the articulations of reality: a judicious use of the universal 'calculator' gives it access to all the secrets of the *machina mundi*, on all levels. Frances Yates comments: 'The Theatre is thus a vision of the world and of the nature of things seen from a height, from the stars themselves, and even from the super-celestial founts of wisdom beyond them.' Like Ficino's *figura mundi* the *Theatro* is also a structure which uses the energy of forces which are contained in the magico-astrological images.[32]

Nevertheless, as they result more and more in memorative techniques and in systems of signs adapted to construct 'machines' capable of organising the memory, the astrological 'images' are subjected to a kind of process of demystification. And it is indeed in this direction which Giordano Bruno seems to be moving. Frances Yates wrote: 'Bruno's effort cannot solely be explained by an interpretation which points to him as being someone who forecast an electronic brain. The divine had not been banished from the hermetic universe in which Bruno lived.' This is in fact true; the echo of hermeticism survives in his work but it is greatly altered.[33] Without a doubt the *De umbris idearum* makes use of the images of the 'decans' for its 'wheels', but it strips them of occultism for the sake of the functioning of the mnemonic systems. Obviously Bruno, who transcribed whole pages of Cornelius Agrippa, inherited from them an aura of mystery. His sources are both hermetic and magico-astrological, nor can his work be read without making constant reference to them. Besides his model is no longer Albumasar; it is Copernicus. It is known that there are also hermetic echoes in Copernicus; but they have a completely different meaning.[34] In the *Spaccio* (Expulsion), the lament of Hermes signifies the vicissitudes of everything, the fatal demise of *all* religions. Here there is an echo of Tycho Brahe's *De nova stella* and of the discussions of the great conjunction in 1583, of Saturn and of Jupiter in the sign of Aries; but there is also his clear wish to bring every extraordinary event back into the rhythm of order and natural law. Bruno looks into the divine coming from nature even when he praises the Egyptians ('the Egyptians, as wise men know, rose up from these natural exteriors of living beasts and plants and . . . penetrated divinity'). In the name of the unity of nature, of the imminence of the divine unity within nature, Bruno condemned the heavens 'divided into so many spheres and then distinguished in forty-eight images', and the imagination of 'foolish mathematicians', and the miraculous. He saw Copernicus as being a liberator, not so much because he put the Sun in place of the Earth as because he destroyed the celestial spheres of the 'foolish mathematicians'. As he says in the *De immenso*: 'The day has come which has destroyed those stars and orbs, and has reduced them to nothing.' ('*Dies illa illuxit, quae ea sidera, et orbes / sustulit, inque suum nihilum . . . resolvit.*') There is no doubt that in Bruno's work we can find the hermeticism, the magic and the astrology of the Renaissance. Only the great liberating experience of Copernicus was decisive for him, and, as Kepler observed, Galileo was now placed at the end of his road. The controversy about astrology was coloured in his work by all the most advanced critical themes so as to be defined in the field of the new science and of a profound moral reform: the 'expulsion of the triumphant beast'.

It was not for this reason that astrology was suddenly to

disappear, linked as it was to conceptions of reality which have not disappeared from modern culture. The Renaissance discussion was instead a decisive contribution which gave a realisation of the methods and foundations to the new scientific knowledge through a clearer distinction between fields, levels and instruments of research: between the rational rigour of the 'sciences' and the 'ideals', the poetic visions, the expectations, the hopes and the faith of men, with all their consequences in life. Without ignoring the fascination of dreams and the effectiveness of the myths, the way to critical reflection and historical research had now been opened up through them.

Notes

Introduction

1 One should also look at Cumont's posthumous volume, *Lux perpetua*, Geuthner, Paris, 1949, and especially pages 303–42, 417–18. As for the astrological codices, besides the *Catalogus codicum astrologorum* by Cumont (Brussels, 12 vols, 1898–1953) it is worth looking at the works presented by Boll and promoted (and partly edited) by F. Saxl and G. Bing, *Verzeichnis astrologischer und mythologischer illustrierter Handschriften des lateinischen Mittelalters*. The first two volumes were published under the auspices of the Heidelberger Akademie der Wissenschaften (Heidelberg, 1915–27); the publication then passed to the Warburg Institute, London (*Catalogue of Astrological and Mythological Illuminated Manuscripts of the Latin Middle Ages*, vols III and IV, 1953–66). See also W. Gundel and H.G. Gundel, *Astrologumena. Die astrologische Literatur in der Antike und ihre Geschichte*, Sudhoffs Archiv Beiheft, 6, Wiesbaden, 1966; F.H. Cramer, *Astrology in Roman Law and Politics*, Memoirs of the American Philosophical Society, 37, Philadelphia, 1954.

2 George Sarton, *Ancient Science and Modern Civilisation*, Harper, New York, 1959, pp. 61ff. See also Lynn Thorndike, 'The True Place of Astrology in the History of Science', *Isis* 46, 1955, pp. 273–8. The same author's great *History of Magic and Experimental Science* (Cambridge University Press, 1923–8, 8 vols) will be systematically referred to below.

3 J. Kepler, *De stella nova*, VIII (*Gesammelte Werke*, ed. Max Caspar, Beck, Munich, 1938, vol. I, pp. 184–6).

4 The theme of the ambiguity of the astrological images, and of 'saving Athens from Alexandria' was underlined by Gertrud Bing

113

in her profile of Aby Warburg (see A. Warburg, *La rinascita del paganesimo antico, Contributi alla storia della cultura raccolti da G. Bing*, La Nuova Italia, Florence, 1966, p. xxxi). On Aby Warburg see Kurt W. Forster, 'Aby Warburg's History of Art: Collective Memory and the Social Mediation of Images', *Daedalus*, Winter 1976, pp. 169–76 (with regard to E.H. Gombrich's work, *Aby Warburg. An Intellectual Biography*, London, 1970).

5 Ernst Mach, *The Science of Mechanics*, tr. T.J. McCormack, Illinois, 1960 (6th ed.), pp. 558–60.

Chapter 1

1 Cf. in particular E. Cassirer, *The Individual and the Cosmos in Renaissance Philosophy*, Blackwell, Oxford, 1963, pp. 98ff. A. Warburg, *La rinascita del paganesimo antico*, La Nuova Italia, Florence, 1966, pp. 247ff, 312ff. Warburg tends, in his celebrated essay of 1920 (in ib., pp. 315–16), to separate Italy from Germany as far as 'divinatory' astrology is concerned. ('The astrology of antiquity had a strange rebirth in Germany, which has not been studied enough to date. The astrological symbols surviving in prophetic literature – above all the seven planets from the human aspect – in fact drew new vigour from that age which was torn apart by social and political struggles and almost became the divinities of the political moment.') Whilst in Italy the 'new artistic-aesthetic conception' of antiquity was to dominate, and the gods of Greece and Rome were to be above all creations of art and beauty ('artistic phenomena'), in Germany, in the climate of the Reformation, predictions and prophecies were to predominate. (D. Cantimori examines this specific point in great detail, 'Note su alcuni aspetti della propaganda religiosa nell'Europa del Cinquecento', in *Aspects de la propagande religieuse*, Droz, Geneva, 1957, pp. 340–51, and in D. Cantimori, *Umanesimo e religione nel Rinascimento*, Einaudi, Turin, 1975, pp. 164–81, to which we must refer for the genesis of a type of research and for bibliographical notes.) Warburg's thesis, which insists that we must 'interpret the figures of Pagan Olympus, which were resurrected in the early Renaissance . . . not as simple artistic phenomena but also as religious beings and study them as such', is valid beyond the Germanic sphere and the atmosphere of the Reformation. 'Pagan augurs' – as he said – 'presented themselves under the guise of scientific erudition' elsewhere too. The claim

114

to separate 'religious' astrology from 'mathematical' astrology precisely is vain and insubstantial.

2 Ptolemy, *Tetrabiblos*, I, 1, tr. F.R. Robbins, Loeb Classical Library, London, etc., 1940 (with Manetho, *Aegyptiaca*). In Isidore of Seville, *Etym.*, III, 27 (ed. Lindsay), we read: 'There is however some difference between Astronomy and Astrology. For Astronomy comprises the revolution of the heavens, the rising, setting and movements of the stars or the causes from which they are so called. But Astrology is partly natural, partly superstitious. It is natural while it follows the courses of the sun and moon or certain fixed positions of the stars in time. But that which the mathematicians follow, who make prophecies on the stars, and who dispose the twelve signs of the zodiac over the individual members of the body or soul, and try to predict the births and characters of men from the course of the stars, is superstitious.' For the connection with magic in general and all the 'prophetic' arts, cf. *Etym.*, VIII, 9. The distinction was to become a topos in medieval literature. For the Oriental world but with plenty of general information and a rich bibliography see C.A. Nallino, 'Raccolte di scritti editi e inediti', vol. V, *Astrologia, astronomia, geografia*, Istituto per l'Oriente, Rome, 1944, pp. 1–87.

In the *Speculum astronomiae* generally attributed to Albertus Magnus (but by some to Roger Bacon), the distinction is immediately fixed 'in theoricam scilicet et practicam' ('namely in the theoretical and the practical') (chs 1–3): 'There are two great kinds of wisdom, each of which is known by the name of astronomy: the first lies in the science of the figure of the first heaven etc. . . . The second great wisdom which is similarly called 'astronomy' is the science of the judgments of the stars, which is the natural tie between philosophy and mathematics.' For fuller information with exhaustive references to the work of Roger Bacon see I. Agrimi and C. Crisciani, 'Albumazar nell'astrologia di Ruggero Bacone', *Acme* 25, 1972, pp. 315–38.

3 Ibn Khaldun, *The Muqaddimah: An Introduction to History*, trans. from the Arabic by Franz Rosenthal, Routledge and Kegan Paul, London, 1958, vol. I, p. 226.

4 E. Cassirer, op.cit., p. 118.

5 A. Warburg, op.cit., p. 371.

6 Pomponazzi, *De naturalium effectuum causis sive de incantationibus*, 12, in *Opera*, Basel, 1567, pp. 266–7: 'Quidam recentes multis verbis ornatis insectantes Astrologos eodem peccato laborant, quo et Averrois; aut enim Astrologos non intelligunt, aut

si intelligunt graviter errant, et certe in illis suis libris non video nisi arrogantiam et petulantiam, et praeter ornatum nihil boni contineri, quanquam aliqui referant sententiam non esse suam, sed tantum ornatum apposuisse.' ('Certain recent writers following the Astrologers with much ornate diction labour under the same mistake as Averroës; for either they do not understand the Astrologers or, if they do, they are seriously in error, and certainly I see in their books only arrogance and impudence and nothing good besides the ornament, though some say that the opinion is not theirs, but they have added so much ornament.') There is a footnote in the margin of Gratarol's edition for Perna: 'Contra Picum Mirandulanum' ('Against Pico della Mirandola'). Pomponazzi himself attacked Pico's *Disputationes*, as is generally known, accusing him of plagiarism perhaps of Savonarola, or did he want above all to attack his nephew Gianfrancesco Pico for his many writings against 'naturalistic' theories of prediction (and his acknowledged opponent on the question of immortality)? There seems to me little doubt that it was the defensive work of Gianfrancesco, with its revival of Sextus Empiricus, which renewed and embittered the controversy over astrology.

7 G.M. Bose, *Sympathiam attractioni et gravitati substituit . . .*, Ex Officina Schlomachiana, Wittenberg [1757], p. xi. Bose referred to the famous work of Albohazen Haly filius Abenragel, *De iudiciis*, Impr. per Bernardinum de Vitalibus, Venice, 1523 (but already published in 1485 and in 1503, composed during the first half of the eleventh century and translated from the Arabic for Alfonso of Castille, into Castilian, and then into Latin around 1256).

8 Bonaventura Cavalieri to Evangelista Torricelli (14 July 1642) in *Discepoli di Galileo. Carteggi*, vol. I, ed. P. Galluzzi and M. Torini, Barbera, Florence, 1976, p. 18.

9 Petrarch, *Rerum senilium*, I, 6 (7) in *Opera omnia*, S. Henricpetri, Basel, 1581, pp. 747–8. See also *Rerum senilium*, III, 1 (to Boccaccio), in *Opera*, pp. 765–72. Thorndike's treatment in *History of Magic and Experimental Science*, Cambridge University Press, 1923–8, III, pp. 213–23) is extraneous, and does not examine in depth the problem of the development of Petrarchan thought nor the variations of themes and emphasis.

10 J. Kepler, *De stella nova in pede Serpentarii . . .*, VIII (in *Gesammelte Werke*, ed. Max Caspar, vol. I, Beck, Munich, 1938, pp. 184–94; *Harmonice mundi*, IV, 7; V, 10 (in *Gesammelte Werke*, ed.cit., vol. VI, Munich, 1940, pp. 266–7, 366). For the questions

touched on here one should also consult the texts referred to fully in S. Tangherlini, 'Tempi platonici e pitagorici nel l' "Harmonice mundi" di Keplero', *Rinascimento* XIV, 1974, pp. 117–78.

11 Galileo, *Opere*, Favaro, Barbera, Florence, 1968, vol. V., pp. 302–5. On the cabbalistic theory of light see S.G. Scholem, *Kabbalah*, 1978, New American Library. (Also the selections from the *Zohar*, edited also by Scholem, Schocken Books, New York, 1966, pp. 29ff. and finally his *On the Kabbalah and its symbolism*, Schocken, 1969). For the Cabbalistic 'fashion' in Florence in the second half of the sixteenth century, from the Florence Academy to Cabbalistic symbols in the Palazzo Vecchio see my essay in *Rinascite e rivoluzioni*, Laterza, Bari, 1975, pp. 43–7.

12 Pietro d'Abano, *Lucidator*, Par. lat. 2598, fol.119r a.

13 For these texts from Pomponazzi I am grateful for Franco Graiff's transcriptions. He is publishing a study of Pomponazzi, begun as a degree thesis, under the supervision of Paola Zambelli at the University of Florence.

14 One can now find essential information on this subject, with the necessary bibliographical detail, in the introduction by M.-Th. d'Alverny and F. Hudry to al-Kindi's 'De radiis', *Archives d'histoire doctrinale et littéraire du Moyen-Age*, Vrin, Paris, 1975, pp. 139–260. One must also remember the 'dances' of the stars refer back to *Timaeus* 40c, and to the commentary of Proclus (ed. Diehl, Teubner, Leipzig, 1906, III, p. 151): 'The eclipses and reappearances of the stars which take place at fixed times indicate the renovation [*apokatastaseis*] of the cosmos and the beginnings of cycles. It is through such phenomena that worldly things are transformed and changed . . . Plato says that the configurations and the movements of heavenly bodies give rise to terror and provide signs of events to those who know the calculations. Thus he lets us know that these phenomena are signs, as is obvious, and signs capable of indicating certain events.' On heavenly 'signs' Plotinus writes very effectively (*Enn.* II, 3, 7, ed. Henry-Schwyzer, 1964): 'The stars are like letters which inscribe themselves at every moment in the sky, or written once for all and self-moving . . . Everything in the world is full of signs . . . All events are co-ordinated . . . Se we find signs of the future in the flight of birds or in other animals. All things depend on each other; as has been said, "everything breathes together" [sympnoia mia].' On the subject of 'rebirth' and 'reform' we allude, in the text, among others, to the volumes of the monumental work by Karl Burdach, *Vom Mittelalter zur Reformation*, which was

published in Berlin between 1913 and 1939.

15 Pseudo-Ovid, *De vetula*, ed. Dorothy M. Robathan, Amsterdam, 1968, p. 130, bk III, vv. 590ff. The connection between astrology, knowledge of a fixed law of nature (I, 229: 'legem naturae fixam ponamus . . .' 'we assert that the law of nature is fixed') and the happiness of the knowledgeable, is noteworthy. Ptolemy's famous epigram, where he contrasts the transient earthly nature of man with his ascent to Zeus while he contemplates and measures the movements of the heavens, also makes reference to astronomy. See F. Boll, *Vita contemplativa* . . ., Sitzungsberichte der Heidelberger Akademie der Wissenschaften, Philos.-hist. Klasse, 1920, 8. Abhandlung, p. 34, n.15.

16 In *De causa Dei*, I, 1, coroll. pars. 35 (opera . . . Henrici Savilii, ex officina Nortoniana apud Ioannem Billium, 1618, pp. 73–4, facsimile repr. Frankfurt, 1964) Bradwardine quotes from *De vetula*, with regard to the thesis 'concerning the great conjunctions of this kind' ('de huiusmodi magnis coniunctionibus'), the specific theory of the birth of Christ, transcribing completely verses 611–44 of the third book, as a preliminary to the comparative analysis – of great interest – of the astrological figurations of the Virgin.

17 *De vetula*, III, 227–32, 363–4 (pp. 258, 263).

18 G. Bruno, *The Expulsion of the Triumphant Beast*, tr. A.D. Imerti, Rutgers University Press, New Brunswick, 1964, p. 241. It is the famous hermetic apocalypse of *Asclepius*, 24 (*Corpus Hermeticum*, ed. A.D. Nock, A.-J. Festugière, II, 'Les Belles Lettres', Paris, 1945, pp. 326ff.) taken up by St Augustine, *De civitate dei*, VIII, 26 (and later widely known through Augustine). Elsewhere Egypt is the 'image of the heavens', and 'the temple of the whole universe'; its affairs reflect a cosmic rhythm. The experiment of translating in rigorous anthropological terms the astrological theme of the *Liber Hermetis* (found and edited by Gundel in 1936), carried out by Franz Cumont (*L'Egypte des astrologues*, Fondation Egyptologique Reine Elisabeth, Brussels, 1937) has a particular importance and not only in the historiographic sphere. It is a speculative examination of exceptional importance.

19 On the death of Hermes and the *Liber Alcidi* see my essay 'Una fonte ermetica poco nota', *La Rinascita*, III, 1940, pp. 202ff. (*Corpus Hermeticum*, ed.cit., IV, 1954, p.146), and in *Studi sul platonismo medievale*, Le Monnier, Florence, 1958, pp. 89–145. On the death and resurrection of cities, Cincius Romanus wrote:

'cities grow old and die like men, yet although it is possible for cities to become worn out with age or dead, the works of men are rejuvenated or brought back to life.' 'Ricerche sulle traduzioni di Platone . . .', in *Medioevo e Rinascimento. Studi in onore di Bruno Nardi*, Sansoni, Florence, 1955, vol. I, pp. 369–70). On Pletho see *Rinascite e rivoluzioni*, pp. 113–20.

20 Ibn Khaldun, op. cit., vol. II, pp. 269–71.
21 R. Lemay, *Abu Ma'shar and Latin Aristotelianism in the Twelfth Century*, Beirut, 1962. For the astrological texts, and the authors quoted here, besides the volume by Nallino indicated above, permit me to refer to my commentary on Giovanni Pico della Mirandola, *Disputationes*, 2 vols, Vallecchi, Florence, 1946–52. For the influence of Albumasar in the Byzantine world see Albumasar, 'De revolutionibus nativitatum', ed. David Pingree, Teubner, Leipzig, 1968. (Pingree published the critical edition of the Greek version. On the sources see Boll's classical work, *Sphaera. Neue Griechische Texte und Untersuchungen zur Geschichte der Sternbilder*, Teubner, Leipzig, 1903. On Albumasar's 'translations' cf. O. Neugebauer, *The Exact Sciences in Antiquity*, Copenhagen, etc., 1951, p. 176, which should be used with some caution.)
22 B.L. Ullman and Ph. A. Stadter, *The Public Library of Renaissance Florence. Niccolò Niccoli, Cosimo de' Medici and the Library of San Marco*, Antenore, Padua, 1972, pp. 208–9 (no. 737 contains apart from the *Introduction Albumasaris*, Ptolemy's *Tetrabiblos*, *Homar Thyberiadis de nativitatibus*, *Alphagranus in scientia astrorum et radicibus motuum coelestium* . . ., Messahallah etc. – now in Florence Biblioteca Nazionale, Conv. Soppr. J, II, 10). But see also p. 212, the astrological anthology (now in the Laurentian Library, Florence) with the 'Flores Albumasar', while an 'Albumasar de revolutione annorum mundi' (ib., p. 211, n.755) has not been traced.
23 Ibn Khaldun, op.cit., vol. II, pp. 211–13. For the other authors see the commentary to Pico, op.cit., I, pp. 636ff.
24 For the authors mentioned here, apart from the commentary to Pico's *Disputationes*, already mentioned, which contains full references, cf. in particular, Pierre d'Ailly, *Concordantia astronomie cum theologia*, Augusta, 1490, with other works (the text cited above is in the *Vigintiloquium*, verb. 5, on which see also Lynn Thorndike, *History*, vol. IV, p. 105. With regard to *De concordia astronomicae veritatis et narrationis historicae* (or *Concordantia astronomiae cum historica narratione*) Kepler

the astrologer himself said [*liber quadrip*, 1, 2, ap. Thomam, *Summa contra gentiles*, III, 86]: "The judgments I give you are between the necessary and the contingent." He also said [*Centiloquium sive aphorismi*, aph.5]: "The astrologer should not say anything with a particular reference but speak universally, because the soul of the wise man will dominate the stars".

4 Coluccio Salutati, *Epistolario*, ed. F. Novati, Istituto Storico Italiano, Rome, 1891, vol. I, pp. 279–83. The *De fato, fortuna et casu*, still unedited, is preserved in numerous manuscripts (including Laur.Conv. soppr.452; Laur.53, 18; Laur.90 sup.42; Vat. lat 1928); on this, and on the astrological and geomantic part, cf. Garin, *I trattati morali di C.S.*, 'Accademia fiorentina di Scienze Morali "La Columbaria" ', II, Le Monnier, Florence, 1944, pp. 29–36 (edn of the geomantic part). On Cecco d'Ascoli, and his astrological writings, see L. Thorndike, *History of Magic and Experimental Science*, Cambridge University Press, 1923–8, vol. II, pp. 948–68. Benvenuto da Imola's commentary on the twentieth canto of Dante's *Inferno* includes the interesting appeal to Averroës: 'I state therefore with Averroës: astrology is nothing of our time. But an astrologer once said: Averroës does not know astrology, but the stars do not lie.' The same type of argument can be found, with Averroës's refutation, in Galeotto Marzio's *De incognitis vulgo*.

5 Coluccio Salutati to Luigi de' Gianfigliazzi (from Stignano, 27 February 1366) in Salutati, *Epistolario*, vol. I, pp. 15–20. On Paolo dell'Abbaco see L. Thorndike, *History*, vol. III, pp. 205–12.

6 Thorndike wrote (*History*, vol. II, p. 836) that if the *Liber astronomicus* by Guido Bonatti de Forlivio was probably the most eminent work of the century, the fullest geomantic text was also by an Italian, the vast *Summa* completed at Bologna in 1288 by Bartolomeo da Parma ('The Art of Geomancy which teaches men to resolve all questions on which they wish to be informed by divine power through that art . . .') For the fortune of the geomancy attributed to Pietro d'Abano, and translated (ed.1542) by Tricasso Mantovano (Patrizio Tricasso da Cerasari) during the sixteenth century, see Thorndike, *History*, vol. V, p. 63. For geomancy in general cf. P. Tannery, 'Le Rabolion . . . Traités de géomancie arabes, grecs et latins' in *Mémoires scientiphiques* published by J.-L. Heiberg, Toulouse–Paris, 1920, vol. IV, pp. 297–411; A. and L. Delatte, 'Un traité byzantin de géomancie', *Mélanges F. Cumont* (Annuaire de l'Institut de Philol. et d'Hist. Orientales et Slaves, IV, 1936), II, pp. 575–658.

7 Ibn Khaldun, *The Muqaddimah: An Introduction to History*, trans. from the Arabic by Franz Rosenthal, Routledge and Kegan Paul, London, 1958, vol. I, p. 230, a text worth reading in its entirety for the subtlety of the analysis.

8 For a fuller analysis and further information on the text cf. Garin, 'Le "Elezioni" e il problema dell'astrologia' in *L'età nuova*, Morano, Naples, 1969, pp. 421–47. Bouché-Leclercq, pp. 458–511 speaks of 'electiones' ('katarchai') as a method in competition, and almost in antithesis, with that of the 'genethliacs'. In fact the continuous circle between heaven and earth explains how they could read equally the movements of the heavens in man, and human events in the sky. (The 'Tabula smaragdina' says: 'What is below is just like what is above, and what is above is just like what is below . . . It ascends from earth to heaven, and then comes back down to earth . . .') It is more difficult to give account of the margin of indeterminateness in which free will introduces its own operation, and the system of mediations through which the unity of the *anima mundi* (soul of the world) is variously explained is very complex. St Thomas, *Summa contra gentiles*, III, 87, observed: 'If therefore the heavenly soul impresses anything on our souls through corporeal motion, that action does not reach our soul except through a change in our body, which indeed is not the cause of our choices, but only the occasion . . . Heavenly motion is not, therefore, the cause of our choice except through the occasion. So the soul of heaven if it is animate, cannot be the cause of our choices or our intelligence through the motion of heavens.' The text by Haly Albohazen filius Abenragel (eleventh century) is derived from 'de iudiciis astrorum' (the Latin translation of which was published in Venice by 1485, and several times subsequently also at Basel). The eighth book of the work 'de electionibus' nevertheless is derived from Zahel, or Sahl b. Bishr (but cf. V. Stegemann, *'Dorotheus von Sidon und die sogenannte 'Introductorium' des Sahl ibn Bishr*, Prague 1942). Zahel wrote in 'de electionibus' on the subject of the harmony between the interrogator and the stars: 'Your choice will be more worthy because you know what will be fitting from the stars.' (As it says in the *Speculum*, II: 'Since nativities are natural things interrogations are like natural things.')

9 Pietro d'Abano, *Lucidator astronomiae*, MS. cit. fol. 100v: 'Ptolemy in the *Quadripartitum* did not speak of interrogations for elections, because, according to the commentary of Hally

Notes to page 47

stellations, and also different ceremonies for operation. Knowledge of all this comes from knowledge of the nature of the stars
and whether the nature of the material harmonises or clashes with
the property of the constellation . . .' On the construction of the
'images', apart from *Picatrix* which we will discuss further, one
should consult Thabit ibn Qurrah, *De imaginibus*, the Latin
translations of which were published by F. Carmody in 1960 (*The
Astronomical Works of Thabit. b. Qurrah*).

16 Ibn Khaldun, op.cit., III, pp. 164ff. For further information and
bibliography see my 'Un manuale di magia: "Picatrix" ' in *L'età
nuova*, op.cit., pp. 387–419. There are not many other texts on
this subject to recommend (in fact many second-hand compil-
ations are to be ignored). Particularly notable is H. Corbin, *En
Islam Iranien. Aspects spirituels et philosophiques*, II, Galli-
mard, Paris, 1971, pp. 300ff. But see also H. and R. Kahane, A.
Pietrangeli, 'Picatrix and the Talismans', *Romance Philosophy*,
XIX, 1965–6, pp. 574–93; F. Rico, *El pequeño mundo del hombre.
Varia fortuna de una idea en las letras españolas*, Editorial
Castalia, Madrid, 1970, pp. 76ff. ('The picturesque miscellany of
astral magic which Alfonso X had translated into Castilian in
1256, was then translated from Castilian into Latin, and so circulated for centuries under the title of *Picatrix*.') For the text, I
have followed Ritter and Plessner's translation from the Arabic
('*Picatrix.' Das Ziel der Weisen von Pseudo-Magriti*, translated
into German from the Arabic by Hellmut Ritter and Martin
Plessner, The Warburg Institute, London, 1962) and the Latin
version which is given in Par.lat.10272 and Magl.XX, 20. A full
study of the Latin text, with an introduction, by V. Perrone
Compagni, is now contained in *Medioevo. Rivista di storia della
filosofia medievale* I, 1975, pp. 237–337.

17 Cf. also *Recueil de plus Célèbres astrologues et quelques hommes
doctes faict par Symon de Phares*, published by Dr E. Wickers-
heimer, Champion, Paris, 1929, p. 36: 'Picatrix was at that time
the most excellent astrologer known, according to some, in the
world, and he demonstrates it well at the beginning of his book,
which is a vast *summa*, even though there are, in fact, in this
book, several sinister things which are prohibited now, but were
not then, though bad teaching was prohibited by it at all times.
This man cites several astrologers whom I shall pass over for the
sake of brevity, because I do not remember them perfectly and
because I have only passed through his work, since it is scholarly.'
(This last remark is a precious testimony to the diffusion of

126

Picatrix during the fifteenth century.) One reads: 'Picatrix, the Spaniard, or the author of the book sent to Alfonso, under the name of Picatrix', in the French fifteenth-century translation of *De praestigiis daemonum* by Johann Wier, the pupil of Cornelius Agrippa (*Histoires disputes et discours des illusions et impostures des diables, des magiciens infames*, Aux bureaux du Progrès médical, Paris, 1885, vol. I, p. 178.

18 *Picatrix*, I, 6 (trans. Plessner, pp. 35–8); but for certain themes, cf. the text cited by G.F. Pico, '*Almadel*' *auctor pseudonymus: de firmitate sex scientiarum*, published from a unique Laurentian manuscript by R.A. Pack, 'Archives d'Histoire Doctrinale et Littéraire du Moyen Age', 42, 1975, Paris, 1976, pp. 147–81.

19 *Picatrix*, IV, 3 (trans. cit. pp. 254–5).

20 *Picatrix*, III, 6 (trans. cit. pp. 198ff., Corbin, op.cit., p. 301).

21 Cod. Arundel 263, 155r, tr. J.P. Richter, 'The Literary Works of Leonardo da Vinci', Oxford, 1939, vol. II, p. 324.

Chapter 3

1 J. Decarreaux, *Les Grecs au Concile de l'Union. Ferrara–Florence 1438–39*, ed. A. and I. Picard, Paris, 1970, p. 106. For the reaction against Aristotelianism, see the characteristic text which J. Gill (The Council of Florence, Cambridge, 1959, p.227) cites, translating from Syropoulos: 'He [one of the Georgian envoys] said, "What about Aristotle, Aristotle? A fig for your fine Aristotle." And when I by word and gesture asked: "What is fine?" the Georgian replied: "St Peter, St Paul, St Basil, Gregory the Theologian; a fig for your Aristotle, Aristotle." '

2 On Pletho's paganism see Milton V. Anastos, 'Pletho's Calendar and Liturgy', *Dumbarton Oaks Papers*, IV, 1948, p. 269. Anastos records how for Gemistus, Christians were only 'sophistai'.

3 This is the well-known text *Comparationes phylosophorum Aristotelis et Platonis*, Per Jacobum Pentium de Leuco, Venice, 1523 (see especially bk III, chapters 11–19, and for the entire question see my work *Rinascite e rivoluzioni*, Laterza, Bari, 1975, pp. 113–19).

4 *Nomoi*, III, 35, 7 and 9 (in Pléthon, *Traité des lois*, ed. G. Alexandre, Didot, Paris, 1858, pp. 208–10, reprinted Amsterdam, 1966). On Pletho's liturgy it is worth looking at Anastos's study, op.cit., pp. 189–305.

5 *Nomoi*, II, 6 (ed.cit. pp. 64ff). Cf. also the whole of 'de differ-

certainly refer to R. Klibansky, E. Panofsky, F. Saxl, *Saturn and Melancholy*, London and New York, 1964 (a revised edition of the famous book by Erwin Panofsky and Fritz Saxl, *Dürers 'Melencolia. I'. Eine quellen- und typengeschichtliche Untersuchung*, Teubner, Leipzig, 1923, which opened the first series of the 'Studien der Bibliothek Warburg'); A. Chastel, *Marsile Ficin et l'art*, Droz-Giard, Geneva–Lille, 1954 is full of important contributions.

20 A. Chastel, op.cit., p. 42.

21 Ficino, *De vita*, III, 11.

22 Ficino, *De vita*, III, 19 and 22.

23 Ficino, *De vita*, III, 19: *On making a figure of the universe . . .* 'Let him carve . . . a certain archetypal form of the world if it pleases him in bronze, which he should then impress on a gilded sheet of silver at an opportune moment . . .'

24 R. Starrabba, *Ricerche storiche su Guglielmo Raimondo Moncada ebreo convertito siciliano del secolo XV*, Tip. Virzi, Palermo, 1878, p. 74 (Archivio Storico Siciliano, NS III, 1878, pp. 85–8; cf. I. Carini, 'Guglielmo Raimondo Moncada', ibid., XXII, 1898, pp. 485–6): ' "de imaginibus coelestibus": haec est illa scientia divina quae felices homines reddit, et ut dii inter mortales videantur edocet: haec est quae cum astris loquitur et, si majus dicere fas est, cum Deo ipso quidquid in mundo est gubernatur . . .' (from Vat.Urb.lat.1384). As is well known, Guglielmo Raimondo Moncada has been identified with Flavius Mithridates. With regard to Mercurio da Correggio and Arquato's prophecy, I would be permitted to refer to my previous works (and in particular to *L'età nuova*, already cited). See also C. Vasoli, *Profezia e ragione*, Morano, Naples, 1974 (and now, David B. Ruderman, 'Giovanni Mercurio da Correggio's Appearance in Italy as seen through the Eyes of an Italian Jew', *Renaissance Quarterly*, 28, 1975, pp. 309–22).

Of great interest is the use Sigismondo Tizio (1458–1528) makes of the astrologers in his *Historiae Senenses* (which I read in the copy of the Biblioteca Nazionale di Firenze, II.V. 140), where Arquarto is also used (besides Paul of Middelburg, Domenico Maria Novara and Regiomontano). Tizio wrote, amongst other things, 'From the conjunction of two superior beings, which occurred in 1484 in the sign of Scorpio, on account of which almost all Italy was then overthrown by the invasion of the French, mathematicians had often predicted that a new lesser prophet would appear when there was a minor conjunction . . .

Paul of Middelburg noted down all this with his judgment, and others agreed with his opinion, supported by the authority of Albumasar and Messahalla . . . that false . . . Antichrist will be a greater prophet springing from the moving conjunction of three bodies in the first degree of Aries; but this lesser conjunction of which we speak was in the sign of Scorpio. Therefore if we have any skill in stars, we shall assert that this lesser prophet was Girolamo Savonarola.'

25 Ficino's famous text on Savonarola-Antichrist was reproduced by Kristeller in *Supplementum ficinianum*, op.cit., II. pp. 76–9. (It had already been edited by Passerini in *Giornale storico degli Archivi toscani*, III, 1859, pp. 115ff.) Ficino too appeals to the astrologers: 'This is not the place to discuss the arguments with which the mathematicians and Platonists contend that Savonarola was inspired by many diverse or unlucky influences from the stars.' On Ficino's *Apologia* see E. Sanesi, *Vicari e canonici e il 'caso Savonarola'*, Libreria Editrice Fiorentina, Florence, 1932, pp. 11–19.

26 Cf. Giancarlo Zanier, 'Il problema astrologico nelle prime opere di Giovanni Pico della Mirandola', *La Cultura*, VIII, 1970, pp. 524–51, many of whose propositions appear somewhat tenuous. If we accept the conclusions of Michele Fuiano, 'Astrologia ed umanesimo in due prefazioni di Andrea di Trebisonda', *Atti dell'Accademia Pontaniana*, NS XVII, 1967–8, pp. 385–412, to which the only objections are chronological difficulties, which are perhaps not insuperable, one could demonstrate that contemporaries already understood the young Pico's positions in different ways. But see also P. Zambelli, 'Platone, Ficino e la magia', in *Studia Humanitatis*. Ernesto Grassi zum 70. Geburtstag, herausgegeben von R. Hora and E. Kessler, W. Fink, Munich, 1973, pp. 121–42.

27 The controversy over astrology, inflamed with such vigour by Pico, cannot be undervalued, except for its singular historical dullness. Theologians, philosophers, scientists participated in it. Through Pomponazzi, Kepler and Mersenne joined in. Though the essential bibliographical data can be found in Thorndike, a detailed work on the subject is lacking. One can find useful information on such a vast subject in P. Zambelli, 'Giovanni Mainardi e la polemica sull'astrologia' in *L'opera e il pensiero di Giovanni Pico della Mirandola nella storia dell'Umanesimo*, Convegno Internazionale 1963, Istituto Naz. di Studi sul Rinascimento, Florence, 1965, vol. II, pp. 205–79. (But see also pp. 315–

31 of the same volume, P. Rossi, 'Considerazioni sul declino dell'astrologia agli inizi dell'età moderna', where among other things L. Thorndike's essay, 'The true place of Astrology in the History of Science', *Isis*, 46, 1955, pp. 273–8 is discussed.) One also would wish to mention here some of the most notable works which the debate inspired: Petrus Garsias, *Determinationes magistrales contra conclusiones etc.*, E. Silber, Rome, 1489; G. Savonarola, *Tractato contra li astrologi*, B. de' Libri, Florence, 1497; Lucius Bellantius, *De astrologica veritate, et in disputationes Io.Pici responsiones*, G. de Haerlem, Florence, 1498; G.F. Pico, *De rerum praenotione* (perhaps already finished by 1502; ed. Strasburg 1506/1507); G.F. Pico, *Quaestio de falsitate astrologiae* (1505/1514; ed. W. Cavini, *Rinascimento*, NS, XIII, 1973, pp. 133–171). For Pontano and his *De rebus coelestibus*, see B. Soldati, *La poesia astrologica nel Quattrocentro. Ricerche e studi*, Sansoni, Florence, 1906. For some aspects of the Pichian debate see now H. de Lubac, *Pic de la Mirandola*, Aubier-Montaigne, Paris, 1974, pp. 307–26.

Chapter 4

1 Pomponazzi, *De naturalium effectuum causis sive de incantationibus*, 12, in *Opere*, Basel, 1567, pp. 266–7. Cf. the French edition with an important introduction and notes by Henri Busson (P. Pomponazzi, *Les Causes des merveilles de la nature ou les enchantements*, Editions Rieder, Paris, 1930, p. 245).

2 R. Ridolfi, *Vita di Girolamo Savonarola*, Sansoni, Florence, 1974, vol. II, p. 550. On Nesi see the essay (with texts) by C. Vasoli, 'Giovanni Nesi tra Donato Acciaiuoli e Girolamo Savonarola. Testi editi e inediti', *Memorie Domenicane*, NS, 4, 1973, pp. 103–79.

3 I owe the reference to the anti-Pico remark to a kind communication from Aleksandr Ch. Gorfunkel (Leningrad, 20 February 1974).

4 On the significance of Gianfrancesco Pico della Mirandola see the volume by C.B. Schmitt, *Gianfrancesco Pico della Mirandola (1469–1533)*, M. Nijhoff, The Hague, 1967, with a full bibliography (for the relationship with Giovanni Mainardi, the famous doctor, see pp. 14–15 and notes).

5 *Disputationes adversus astrologiam divinatricem*, XII, 3 (ed. Garvi, vol. II, Vallecchi, Florence, 1946, pp. 498–500) but it is

worth looking at the entire twelfth book from which the passages referred to are taken.

6 *Disputationes*, XII, 3 (op.cit., vol. II, p. 500).

7 In this respect a precise comparison with Nicholas of Cusa, not only on general themes but on precise attitudes, would be interesting. In *'de coniecturis'*, I, 1 (*Opera omnia*, III, ed. J. Koch, C. Bormann, Jo. G. Senger), in comparison with God and the animals, man, or more precisely, the 'mens' (mind) of man, has a precise nature, as 'coniecturalis mundi forma' ('the form of the conjectural world'). ('As that absolute divine entity is everything which is in whatever it is, so the unity of the human mind is the entity of its conjectures. God, however, causes everything by means of himself, since he is equally the beginning and end of all things, so the explanation of the rational world proceeding from our complex mind is caused by means of this [mind] as creator.') As God is the creative unity of the real world, man is the totality of the 'symbolic' world of 'conjectures'.

8 Only a certain historiographic obtuseness, and the inadequate penetration of texts that are more often catalogued than read (Thorndike's great work, for example, is a catalogue and index rather than a history), obscures the significance of the Pichian polemic, which indeed forced all his contemporaries to take up positions. As far as the place of astrology in everyday life is concerned, the discussion is a long one, and still largely to be done.

9 For the influence of the astrological debate on the medical field, the collection of texts gathered by Troilo Lancetta [Lootri Nacattel] in his *Raccolta medica et astrologica*, published by the Guerigli press in Venice in 1645. The volume contains in the vernacular the texts by Fracastoro on critical days, and a full collection of the writings of Cremonini (as well as passages from Greek authors). It is a characteristic document of the astrological debate in the medical field, as it came to be defined in the seventeenth century.

10 On Pontano, as well as the literature linked to him, see F. Tateo, *Astrologia e moralità in G. Pontano*, Adriatica, Bari, 1960, and now Mauro De Nichilo, *I poemi astrologici di Giovanni Pontano. Storia del testo*, Dedalo, Bari, 1975.

11 On Cornelius Agrippa, on magic (and astrology) and also for the bibliographical information it contains see P. Zambelli, 'Le problème de la magie naturelle à la Renaissance', in *Magia, astrologia e religione nel Rinascimento*, 'Convegno polacco-italiano,

Varsavia 25–27 September 1972', Wroclaw–Warsaw–Krakow–
Danzig, 1974, pp. 48–82 (also for the references to many preceding
contributions and editions of texts by Agrippa, by the same
Zambelli). Cf. Wayne Shumaker, *The Occult Science in the
Renaissance. A Study in Intellectual Patterns*, University of
California Press, Berkeley–Los Angeles–London, 1972.

12 On the subject of Benivieni and Cattani I may be permitted
to refer (apart from Busson's introduction to his anthological
version of *De incantationibus*) to what I wrote many years ago in
Medioevo e Rinascimento, Laterza, Bari, 1973, 4th ed.

13 The subtle and complex relationship between Ficino and Pomponazzi has never been adequately clarified. Chapter X of *De
incantationibus* is, nevertheless, illuminating (especially if it is
reread in the original text of the manuscripts without the small
but insidious interpolations of Gratarol). For Pomponazzi,
Plato's (Ficino's) positions do not differ substantially from those
of the Peripatetics – he has different preoccupations. Aristotle
(together with the Aristotelians) knows that to the ignorant herd
(*homines non philosophi, qui revera sunt veluti bestiae*) ('men
not philosophers who in truth are like beasts') one cannot tell
'scientific' truth. ('They cannot understand that God, the
Heavens and Nature can cause these things, and so they believe
that [they are from] intelligent beings as if from men – for they
can only understand corporeal things – so angels and demons are
introduced, although those who introduce them can understand
them least of all.') Fables, spirits and 'the mystical senses' have
thus been introduced with a practical purpose, '*propter ignavum
vulgus*' ('for the ignorant herd'). 'For the language of religions, as
Averroës says in his *Poetics*, is like the discourse of the poets. Such
fables serve to lead us to truth, and instruct the ignorant rabble
that it is right to aim at good and shun evil, just as one does with
children by the hope of reward and the fear of punishment.' For
this reason Pomponazzi maintains ('he is not alien to me, nor far
from the truth') that Plato 'introduced angels and demons, not
because he believed in their existence, but because his purpose
was to instruct common men.' In fact, as Aesculapius was a
doctor of bodies, 'so Plato was [a doctor] of human souls'. (Here
Pomponazzi clearly takes up Ficino's theme of the relationship
between the medicine of the body and 'platonic' medicine of the
soul, and of the 'conversion' of Ficino himself from medicine to
Platonism. Aristotle, instead, oriented towards 'science', did not
take refuge in metaphor, but nor did he openly risk discussions

which could arouse the suspicion of the priests ('on these matters little or nothing'), who had already killed Socrates ('since this position totally removed the Gods'). Plato, who had put forward political and pedagogical aims, who had exalted the good and spoken above all 'through enigmas, metaphors and fables', succeeded in gaining directly a reputation for sanctity ('No wonder that Plato was exalted by the ignorant and by priests'; cf. *De incantationibus*, 10, ed. Gratarol, op.cit, pp. 200–8, with corrections from Arezzo, Biblioteca della Fraternità dei Laici, MS.390 [389]).

Those who collect these similar passages will retain no doubts about either the position of Pomponazzi himself or his judgment about Ficino and Platonism. As for Aristotelianism, of which he declared himself a follower ('My love and the regard I have had for Aristotle from my very youth, impelled me . . .'), his conclusions are explicit: 'since . . . this position totally removed the Gods, he could not safely divulge it through the laws of the Gentiles and others: for states would be destroyed and the priests reduced to nothing. However, their power was always very great. Therefore philosophers were always suspected concerning religion – as Plato mentions in the *Apology*, to such an extent that they were always hated or regarded with derision.'

14 *Libri quinque de fato, de libero arbitrio et de praedestinatione*, ed. Richard Lemay, in Aedibus Thesauri Mundi, Lucani, 1957, II, 7, 1, 44, pp. 205–6; on 'successive vicissitude', on 'successive and perpetual vicissitude', ib. p. 195.

15 *Epilogus sive peroratio*, op.cit., pp. 451–3.

16 *De incantationibus*, X (ed. Gratarol, op.cit., pp. 147–8).

17 *De incantationibus*, X (ib. pp. 149–50).

18 *De incantationibus*, IV (ib. pp. 57–8). The famous Biagio Pelacani da Parma, who was professor at Padua, had given sensational 'natural' explanations of this type. On him as an 'astrologer' see G. Frederici Vescovini, 'Su uno scritto astrologico di Biagio Pelacani da Parma', *Rinascimento*, Second Series, vol.XI, 1971, pp. 79–93.

19 It is worth reading the whole of chapter XII of *De incantationibus* (but see ed.cit. pp. 286–7).

20 *De incantationibus*, XII (ed.cit., p. 284).

21 *De incantationibus*, XII (ib., pp. 286–7): 'Therefore everything today is cold in our faith, and there are no more miracles, unless they are false and deceptive: for the end seems near . . . For no virtue flows down from the heavens except at a certain time . . .

and afterwards their image, broken and useless, remains cold and dead.' For Vanini, cf. Corvaglia's edition of the *Opere* (Soc.An. Ed. Dante Alighieri, 1934), vol. II, pp. 284–93, where the corresponding passages from Pomponazzi are reproduced alongside.

22 Democritus Junior (Robert Burton). *The Anatomy of Melancholy*, III. sect.4, mem.2, subst.1 (Chatto & Windus, London, 1887, pp. 708–9). On the subject of the relationship between Pomponazzi and Mersenne cf. R. Lenoble, *Mersenne ou la naissance du mecanisme*, Vrin, Paris, 1943, pp. 109–21, with the references to *Quaestiones in Genesim* (S. Cramoisy, Lutetiae Parisiorum, 1623); but it is worth looking at Busson's introduction to his translation of *De incantationibus*. Cf. also Giancarlo Zanier, *Ricerche sulla diffusione e fortuna del 'De incantationibus' di Pomponazzi*, La Nuova Italia, Florence, 1975.

23 But a particular commentary was made on 'Theophrastus redivivus', on which see T. Gregory, 'Erudizione e ateismo nella cultura del Seicento. Il 'Theophrastus redivivus', *Giornale critico della Filosofia Italiana*, 51, 1972, pp. 194–240.

24 Nifo wrote a commentary on the *Tetrabiblos* (*Ad Apotelesmata Ptolemaei eruditiones*, Naples, 1513), in which he took up again the debate he had already conducted with Pico in *De nostrarum calamitatum causis* of 1505 ('What Pico says with his peace is nothing'). Particularly influential was his *De falso diluvii prognosticatione* for the 'conjunction' of 1524 (on which see L. Thorndike, *History*, vol. V, pp. 178–233, which examines in general the literature on the conjunction of 1524). Of Cardano's work it is enough to refer to the commentary on the *Quadripartitum* considered by some to be a kind of 'Encomium astrologiae'. On Nifo see P. Zambelli, 'I problemi metodologici del necromante A. Nifo', *Medioeva*, I, 1975, pp. 129–71.

25 Alexandre Koyré, *From the Closed World to the Infinite Universe*, Harper, New York, 1958, pp. 24–7.

26 Marcelli Palingenii Stellati, *Zodiacus vitae*, bk. XI, Aquarius (J. Schweighauser, Basel, 1789), p. 324 (collated with the text of the first Venetian edition of Bernardinus Vitalis).

27 *Zodiacus vitae*, XI, Aquarius, ed.cit., p. 325.

28 *Zodiacus vitae*, XI, Aquarius, ib., pp. 329–30: 'Naturam vero appello legem omnipotentis / supremique patris quam prima ab origine mundi / cunctis imposuit rebus, jussitque teneri / inviolabiliter, dum mundi secla manerent / Nam legem hanc Deus indidit: unde / quum rebus dant esse, Dei mandata libenter / afficiunt formae et nequeunt hanc fallere legem. / Nempe suis res

a formis tales generantur / quales praecipit qui formas condidit ipsas.'

29 *Zodiacus vitae*, XI, Aquarius, op.cit. pp. 330–1: 'At coelum vacuum, vacuum coelo esse putatur? / O vacuae potius mentes, quae credite istud! / quippe suos etiam cives habet aether: et astra / singula sunt urbes coeli, sedesque deorum. / Illic et reges, populi inveniuntur et illic, / sed veri reges, populi veri omnia vera: / non, velut hic, umbrae simulacraque inania rerum . . .'

30 R. Tuve wrote the introduction to the reprint of the English translation by Barnaby Googe (Scholar's Facsimiles and Reprints, New York, 1947), which also had an exceptionally wide circulation as a school textbook. (The French translation by De La Monnerie, *Le Zodiaque de la vie, ou Preceptes pour diriger la Conduite et les Moeurs des Hommes*, Van den Rietoom, A La Haye, 1731, follows the sixteenth-century attempts by Scévole de Sainte-Marthe.) Cf. F. Yates, *Giordano Bruno and the Hermetic Tradition*, Routledge and Kegan Paul, London, 1964, pp. 247ff.

31 *Zodiacus vitae*, XI, Aquarius, ed.cit., pp. 332–3; 'Yet passage have the dwellers there, nothing their course hath barde. / For unto these celestiall states the maiestie divine, / Appointed slendrest bodies hath of substance light and fine, / So that no neede of dores they have, nor yet of windowes wide, / For through the thickest walles they run . . .'

32 Cf. Giulio Camillo, *Tutte le opere*, Gabriel Giolito de Ferrari, Venice, 1552 (and L. Bolzoni, 'Eloquenza e alchimia in un testo inedito di Giulio Camillo', *Rinascimento*, NS, XIV, 1974, pp. 243–67, where *De transmutatione* is published. On Camillo, apart from F. Secret, 'Le cheminements de la Kabbale à la Renaissance. Le Théâtre du monde de G.C.D. et son influence', *Rivista critica di storia della filosofia*, XIV, 1959, pp. 418–36, F. Yates, *The Art of Memory*, Routledge and Kegan Paul, London, 1966, pp. 129–72. The quotations are taken from the first volume of the *Opere*.

33 The dependence of Bruno on Ficino's 'De vita coelitus comparanda' was taken up by contemporaries even to the accusation of plagiarism, as emerged from a remarkable testimony by George Abbot, rediscovered in 1960 by Robert McNulty, 'Bruno at Oxford', *Renaissance News*, XIII, 1960, pp. 300–5 (and F. Yates, *Giordano Bruno*, op.cit., 207–9). See also A. Ingegno, 'In margine al "de immenso" del Bruno', *Rinascimento*, NS X, 1960, pp. 89–115 and above all 'Ermetismo e oroscopo della religioni nello "Spaccio" bruniano', *Rinascimento*, NS XVIII, 1967, pp. 157–74.

34 On Copernicus, Bodin in the *Methodus* (ed. in *Oeuvres Philo-*

sophiques, by P. Mesnard, Presses Universitaires de France, Paris 1951, p. 200) observed: 'He thought the revolutions of the dominions tended towards the centre of a small, eccentric circle and its motion, as his pupils write.' He added: 'Nor did Copernicus dare to write it, but his pupils have handed this dream down as something certain and established.' But on Bodin it would be useful to re-examine whether the whole theory of 'revolutions of kingdoms (*conversiones rerumpublicarum*) is related to the stars and in what way ('God using the stars as instruments') or if it is derived 'from Pythagorean numbers' ('Divine wisdom . . . links all things with wonderful order, motion, number, harmony and form').

Index

Index

Boll, Franz, ix, 25–7, 31, 113, 118–19, 121
Book of Images of Mercury (Hermes), 40
Bose, G.M., 5–6, 116
Bradwardine, Thomas, 17, 65
Brahe, Tycho, 111
Bruni, Francesco, 31
Bruno, Giordano, 18, 48, 81–2, 98, 109, 110–11, 118, 137
Burton, Robert, 104, 136

Cabbalism, 11, 109, 117
Camillo Delminio, Giulio, 108–10, 137
Campanella, Tomaso, 18
Cardano, G., 104, 136
Cassirer, Ernst, xii, 2–5, 114–15
Catalogus codicum astrologum (Cumont), vii–viii, 113
Cattani, Andrea, 97, 134
causes, natural, 81
Cavalieri, Bonaventura, 7, 9, 116
cave image, 53
Celestino, San, 102
Celsus, 59
Centiloquium, 49
'Chaldean Oracles', 59, 61, 72
Chaldeans, 88–90
charlatanism, *see* trickery
Chastel, André, xv, 72, 130
choice, 21
Christianity: and astrology, 22–5, 65, 78, 90, 103; unity of, 56–7; *see also* religion
Cicero, 30
city, ideal, 52
Commentarium in Almagestum (George of Trebizond), 78
Conclusiones (Pico), 45, 78, 85
'concord of the world', *see* unity

conjunctions, great, 15–29 *passim*, 35, 111; *see also* planets
Copernicus, N., xiii, 9, 110–12, 137–8
Corbin, H., 47, 126–7
Corpus Hermeticum, 47, 64, 118, 128
Correggio, Mercurio da, 77, 130
Council for Church Unity, 56, 59
criticism of astrology, 83–112
Cumont, Franz, vii–x, 113, 118, 129
cycles of history, 15, 30, 60, 93, 98–100

D'Agnolo di Giusto, Diotifeci, 64
Dagomari, Paolo, 34
De astrologica veritate (Bellanti), 84, 132
De causa Dei (Bradwardine), 17, 65, 118, 128
De doctrina promiscua (Narni), 44
De fato, de libero arbitrio (Pomponazzi), 98–9
De fato, fortuna et casu (Salutati), 33–4, 122
De incantationibus (Pomponazzi), 5, 83, 96, 98, 124, 135
De magnis coniunctionibus (Albumasar), 20–1
De naturalium effectuum (Pomponazzi), 3, 115
De nova stella (Brahe), 111
De occulta philosophia (Agrippa), 95
De pluviis (al-Kindi), 46
De revolutionibus (Ibn Ezra), 21
De stella nova (Kepler), 116, 120
De umbris idearum (Bruno), 110

140

Index

Index

Index